JOAO DE BARROS

Books of the XCHR Studies Series

No.1 : João de Barros: Portuguese Humanist and Historian of Asia/ *C.R. Boxer*

No. 2 : Coastal Western India: Studies from the Portuguese Records/ *M.N. Pearson*

No. 3 : The Black Legend of Portuguese India: Diogo do Couto, His Contemporaries and the Soldado Prático-A Contribution to the Study of Political Corruption in the Empires of Early Modren Europe/ *George Davison Winius*

No. 4 : Health and Hygience in Colonial Goa (1510-1961)/ *Fátima da Silvà Gracias*

No. 5 : Trade and Finance in Portuguese India: A Study of the Portuguese Country-Trade, 1770-1840/ *Celsa Pinto*

No. 6 : Goa and the Revolt of 1787/ *Charles J. Borges* (Ed.)

No. 7 : Goa and Portugal: Their Cultural Links/ *Charles J. Borges* and *Helmut Feldmann* (Eds.)

No. 8 : Goa-Kanara Portuguese Relations 1498-1763/ *B.S. Shastry* and *Charles J. Borges* (Eds.)

No. 9 : Goa's Foremost Nationalist: José Inácio Candido de Loyola: The Man and His Writings/ *Charles J. Borges* (Ed.)

No. 10 : Goa and Portugal: History and Development/ *Charles J. Borges, Óscar G. Pereira* and *Hannes Stubbe* (Eds.)

No. 11 : Conversions and Citizenry: Goa under Portugal 1510-1610/ *Délio de Mendonca*

About the Author

C.R. Boxer has travelled widely in Asia Africa, and lived for twelve years in the Far East. He is Professor Emeritus of London and Yale Universities, and a fellow of the British Academy of the Lisbon Academy of Science, and of the School of Oriental and African Studies, London.

XCHR Studies Series No. 1

João de Barros

Portuguese Humanist and Historian of Asia

C.R. BOXER

CONCEPT PUBLISHING COMPANY PVT. LTD.
NEW DELHI-110059

ISBN: 978-81-7022-182-1

Edition 2025

Published and Printed by

Concept
Since 1974

Concept Publishing Company Pvt. Ltd.
A/15-16, Commercial Block, Mohan Garden,
New Delhi-110059 (India)
T: 91-11-41101460
E: publishing@conceptpub.com, *W*: www.conceptpub.com

INTRODUCTION

The Xavier Centre of Historical Research has been established to promote high-quality research in the history and culture of Western India, particularly during the period of Portuguese colonialism. It is a matter of pride for the new Centre to initiate its series of XCHR-Studies with a monograph by our veteran historian of the Portuguese empire, Professor C.R. Boxer, whose vastness and depth of approach sets a most desirable tone to our pursuit. Also the choice of the subject, João de Barros, a bureaucrat and a pedagogue, a moralist and a humanist, a linguist and a historian of Portuguese "conquest, navigation and commerce" in the East, provides an excellent backdrop for a more meaningful study of the historical developments in the East from the sixteenth century onwards.

The Centre is grateful to Professor Boxer for his generous offer of the manuscript without any financial consideration, and we are also thankful to Dr. John Correia-Afonso, S.J. for permitting us to publish it in the XCHR-Studies series as a sign of meaningful collaboration between his Heras Institute of Indian History and Culture (Bombay) and the new Xavier Centre of Historical Research, Porvorim, Goa.

PANAJI,
2nd May 1979

DR. TEOTONIO R. DE SOUZA, S.J.
Director
Xavier Centre of Historical Research

PREFACE

The fame of João de Barros (*c.* 1496-1570) both in his own country and abroad, is primarily due to his work as the semi-official chronicler of Portuguese expansion in his *Decades of Asia*. He is one of the relatively few Portuguese to figure in such literary compendia as *The Penguin Companion of European Literature*, where, incidentally, fewer Portuguese authors are listed than Danish, Swedish, Polish and Hungarian.

There are four outstanding sixteenth-century Portuguese chroniclers of Asia. Two of these, Gaspar Correa (149[?]-156[?]) and Diogo do Couto (c. 1542-1616) were the subjects of short but adequate monographs by Aubrey Fitz Gerald Bell some fifty-five years ago. So little is known about the life of the third, Fernão Lopes de Castanheda (149[?]-1559) that it would not be possible to devote more than a couple of pages to his career. João de Barros hitherto has lacked a biographer in English, although he is incontestably the most important of the four.

Inevitably, the emphasis in this book is on Barros as a historian of Portuguese expansion, since that is where his main interest for us lies. But I have devoted some attention to him as a humanist, a moralist, and a pedagogue : although I regard myself as his biographer and his expositor rather than his literary critic.

C.R.B.

ACKNOWLEDGEMENTS

I have to thank the British Academy for a grant which enabled me to finish this book at Lisbon in October and November 1973, in the intervals of archival research on another subject. I am also indebted to various friends and colleagues, including Professors Eugenio Asensio, Luís de Matos, Maria Leonor Carvalhão Buescu and Fernando Castelo-Branco, for stimulating discussion on and clarification of certain points. They are not, of course responsible for such errors of fact and of interpretation that I may have committed inadvertently. Senhora Graça de Almeida Rodrigues was most helpful in securing xerox copies of obscure articles, which I could not obtain in London. The late Senhor Jorge A.M. Rosa typed the manuscript with a speed and accuracy which could not have been bettered. Unforeseen circumstances having prevented the publication of this work in 1974, I am all the more grateful to Fr. John Correia-Afonso S.J., Director of the Heras Institute, for his generous offer to publish it five years later.

CONTENTS

CHRONOLOGY

1495 (27 October)	Accession of King Manuel I.
1496	João de Barros born, in all probability at Viseu, Beira Alta, Portugal.
15??-1520	Serves as a page in the royal household, mostly in the company of the *Infante* Dom João (Prince John).
c. 1521	Marriage with Maria de Almeida.
1521 (December)	Death of King Manuel and accession of King John III.
1522	Publication of *Clarimundo*. Second edition in 1555.
c. 1522-23	Voyage to Mina in Guinea.
1525-28	Serves simultaneously as Treasurer of the Houses of India, Mina, and Ceuta at Lisbon.
1532	Publication of *Ropica Pnefma*.
1533-67	Factor of the India House at Lisbon.
1533	Panegyric to King John III delivered at Evora (published 1740).
1534	André de Resende's inaugural address at Lisbon University (Oct.).
1535	Grant of captaincy in the Brazil-Maranhão.
1535-36	Disastrous failure of the first colonizing expedition which he sent to the Brazil-Maranhão.
1539	*Cartinha com os preceitos e mandamentos da Santa Madre Igreja*.
1540	*Grammatica da Lingua Portuguesa*, which included the better known *Dialogo em louvor da nossa linguagem*.
1540	*Dialogo da viciosa vergonha*.

1540	*Dialogo de preceitos moraes cõ prática delles, em módo de jogo*. Second edition with a slightly different title in 1563.
c.-1540	*Grammatices Rudimenta* (ed. Maria Leonor Carvalhão Buescu, 1972).
*c.*1542-43	*Diálogo Evangélico sobre os artigos da Fé contra o Talmud dos Judeus* (ed. I.S. Révah, 1950).
1545	Panegyric to the Princess Dona Maria (first published, 1655).
1552	*Asia de Joam de Barros dos feitos que os Portugueses fizeram no descobrimento e conquista dos mares e terras do Oriente* (colophon dated 28 June).
1553	*Segunda decada da Asia de Joã de Barros dos feitos que os Portugueses fizeram no descobrimẽto e cõquista dos mares e terras do oriente* (colophon dated 24 March).
1556-61	Second disastrous expedition organized by João de Barros to the Brazil-Maranhão, in which two of his sons participated.
1557	Death of King John III (11 June) ; Regency of Queen Catherine for the infant King Sebastian.
1561	"Abusões do Tempo", or "Exclamação contra os vicios", an unpublished poem of over 460 stanzas completed in this year.
1563	*Terceira decada da Asia de Joam de Barros. Dos feytos que os Portugueses fizeram no descobrimento e conquista dos mares e terras do Oriente* (colophon dated 28 August). A few days earlier, there appeared the second edition of the *Dialogo de João de Barros com dous filhos seus* (colophon dated 20 August).

1567	A paralytic stroke forces his retirement from office to his *quinta* near Pombal.
1568	King Sebastian assumes the government on attaining the age of fourteen.
1570 (21 October)	Death of Barros at his *quinta* of São Lourenço de Litem (also spelt Alitem, Leitem, etc.), and burial in the hermitage-chapel of Santo António.
1577	Three of his heirs refuse to accept their share of his heavily indebted inheritance.
1610	Transference of the remains of Barros to Alcobaça by the Bishop Dom Jorge de Ataide, his godson.
1615	*Quarta Decada da Asia de João de Barros, dos feitos que os Portugueses fizerão no descobrimento e conquista dos mares e terras do Oriente*, edited by João Baptista Lavanha and published at Madrid.

1

THE PORTUGUESE RENAISSANCE AND JOAO DE BARROS

João de Barros began his literary labours in 1520. When he died fifty years later, he left a substantial body of published works and several others in various stages of completion. The half-century of his working life, for most of which he was likewise a busy government official, coincided with the flowering of the Renaissance and of Humanism in Portugal, and with the beginning of their decline. The reigns of King Manuel I (1495-1521) and King John III (1521-57) have generally been regarded as forming the Golden Age of Portugal, both because of the little country's spectacular expansion overseas in that period, as on account of the cultural achievements of Portuguese humanists.

Since João de Barros unquestionably ranks as one of the leading Portuguese humanists, it may be as well to define, albeit rather loosely, in what sense the term is used here. As a rough generalisation, the humanists of sixteenth century Europe may be divided into three main categories : (1) Those who were so devoted to classical scholarship and to copying or adopting Greek and Roman ideals (or what they believed to be such) that they either abandoned Christianity altogether, or else they merely professed it *pro forma*. These Neo Pagans, as they are sometimes termed, were never numerous and were virtually limited to Italy. (2) Those, like Erasmus, whose passion for classical ideals and forms did not demolish their faith in Christianity, but led them to desire extensive and profound reforms in the Church—some to a greater and others to a lesser degree. (3) Those who retained their religious beliefs and orthodoxy in full measure, and who ardently cultivated Greek and Latin literature without being deeply affected by Greek and Roman ideals. The great majority of Portuguese humanists fall within the last category; although, of course, a man might shift from one viewpoint to another, or from one shade of emphasis to another, as his intellectual development or his social surroundings modified his convictions.

The two main influences in the cultural life of Portugal were the royal court and the clergy. During the second half of the fifteenth century, a number of Italian classical scholars had been welcomed at the Portuguese court, including several who tutored members of the royal family. Numbers of Portuguese also went abroad to the Italian universities of Bologna, Siena, Florence and Padua—or even further afield to Paris and Oxford. This was partly because Lisbon University, the only one in Portugal, was a very backward institution with no international prestige. The exodus of Portuguese intellectuals to foreign universities, including those of Spain, where Salamanca was the one which they most frequented, increased in the early decades of the sixteenth-century. Some of these Portuguese pilgrims to the chief centres of cultural life in Western Europe stayed there for good, but the majority returned home sooner or later. By the early sixteenth century there were enough of them, especially at the court, to prepare the way for the generation to which João de Barros belonged and which brought Portuguese humanism to full flower between 1525 and 1557.[1]

A German traveller, Nicholas von Poppelau, who spent a short time at the court of King John II in 1484, was far from favourably impressed. He observed acidulously : "The Portuguese are coarse and ill-natured. They are a brutal people, including those of the king's own household". Ten years later, another German visitor, Sebastian Münzer, received exactly the opposite impression : "The Portuguese of both sexes are a very affable and polite people". Perhaps Nicholas von Poppelau's opinions were coloured by King John II's murder of his brother-in-law, the Duke of Viseu, and by the public execution of the Duke of Braganza on a charge of high treason.[2] In any event, King John II, though no great scholar himself, did know Latin. He had a lively and intelligent mind, and he took the deepest interest in anything that came out of Africa, whether human, animal, vegetable, or mineral. On at least one occasion, he abolished all customs duties on the importation of foreign books, avowedly in order to encourage the dissemination of useful knowledge in his kingdom. Münzer, who was introduced to the king by Cataldo Parisio Siculo, a famous Italian humanist, who was tutor to the king's illegitimate son, Dom Jorge, termed John II "very wise and very learned". The next two monarchs of the House of Aviz continued and expanded the "Perfect Prince's" patronage of learning and of scholars.

King Manuel I established *bolsas* or monetary grants enabling Portuguese students to study in foreign universities, including those of Louvain and Paris; for in the early sixteenth century the focus of humanism began to shift from Italy to France and the Low Countries. King John III, although less intelligent than either Manuel I or John II, was an even greater and more generous patron of learning. In 1527 he made endowments to support fifty Portuguese students at the celebrated Parisian college of St. Barbara (Collége de Sainte Barbe). The principal aim in making these grants was to train a nucleus of highly qualified teachers, particularly theologians, who would raise the standard of education in Portugal on their return. This aim was certainly achieved to a considerable degree. Nearly 300 Portuguese students matriculated at Paris between 1500 and 1550, the great majority of them being *bolseiros del Rei*, whose studies were subsidized by the Crown for a period of up to ten years. There were also *bolseiros* at Louvain and Bordeaux; but the main attraction for many Portuguese students was neighbouring Salamanca, where some 800 were admitted in the first-half of the 16th century, including a few *bolseiros* although the great majority were studying at their own expense, or that of their families, like the celebrated crypto-Jewish physician, Garcia d'Orta (*c.* 1501-1568), who attended both Salamanca and Alcalá de Henares. As mentioned above, not all of these scholars returned home, but the majority did so, thereby raising the quality of Portuguese intellectual life to an appreciable extent.

Among the Portuguese humanists who achieved an international reputation may be mentioned : Aires Barbosa (*c.* 1470-1540), professor of Greek and Latin for twenty years at Salamanca, who later tutored members of the royal family in Portugal; Aquiles Estaço (1524-81), an outstanding Greek and Hebrew scholar, Latin Secretary to successive Popes, and a renowned philological commentator on classical texts; Diogo de Gouveia the elder (1471-1557), successively Rector of the Sorbonne and of the College of St. Barbara. A famous classical scholar, he yet remained a rigidly orthodox Roman Catholic theologian, differing in this respect from some of his nephews, who also taught for long periods at French universities, but who were at one time or another suspected of holding semi-heretical views; António de Gouveia (150?-1565), who taught successively at Toulouse, Avignon, and Cahors, before moving to Turin, where he died; Marcial de Gouveia (1495-15??), famous as a Latin poet, who taught at Poitiers and later at Coimbra; André de Gouveia (150?-1548) who succeeded his uncle at Sainte-Barbe and then became Rector of the College of Guienne at Bordeaux (1534), where he introduced many pedagogical innovations and attracted thither many of his compatriots; Diogo de Gouveia, the younger (15??-1576), who studied at Paris, where he was later Principal of Sainte-Barbe, 1538-44, and taught at Coimbra after being a leading Portuguese theologian at the Council of Trent, 1551-1563.

Less well known abroad, perhaps, but a striking and singularly sympathetic figure, was André de Resende (150?-1573), who studied in Spain, Flanders and France, and became the chief Portuguese propagandist of Erasmus. He tutored several members of the royal family after his return home, and he gave the inaugural address at the University of Lisbon on 1 October 1534.[3] Published in the same month, it breathes the euphoria of the High Renaissance, "when nearly the whole of Europe is being reborn". He urged that Portugal should now follow the example set by Italy, "mother of learning", France, England, Germany, "which at present disputes the palm of letters with Italy", and neighbouring Spain. "For these nations surpass us, not in native genius, nor by virtue of a superior climate, but only and decisively by the care and patience which they devote to academic learning. This is why they daily produce erudite men who with the monuments of their genius attain renown for themselves and immortality for their country. When we read their works we ought truly to feel ashamed of our gross ignorance and our slothfulness." He urged his listeners to study Greek as well as Latin, "since nobody can attain a solid culture without these two languages".

It was André de Resende who was instrumental in bringing the great Flemish humanist, Nicholas Clynaerts (Clenardus, 1493-1542) to Portugal. Professor of Greek and Hebrew, successively at Louvain and Salamanca, he accepted King John III's invitation to come and tutor the (later) Cardinal-Infante Dom Henrique in 1533. He has left us a fascinating picture of the royal court and of Portuguese society as he saw them, but some of his obvious bias must be discounted.[4] One of his pupils at Paris (where he taught for a short time) and Louvain was Fr. Roque de Almeida, a restless Franciscan friar who was the brother-in-law of João de Barros. A true humanist, Clenardus refused to correspond or to converse in any but a classical language, and he even compelled his three Negro slaves to learn Latin. Although often homesick in the Iberian Peninsula for his native Brabant, Clenardus was essentially a cosmopolitan humanist. He was one of those (like Erasmus) who regarded all European classical scholars as their brethren in preference to their own uneducated compatriots. Portuguese humanists, or at any rate those of them who stayed in Portugal, tended to be more nationalistic. They gladly glorified the martial exploits of their countrymen in the East, whether in the Latin of André de Resende and Diogo de Teive, or in the vernacular of João de Barros. If we except such few works as those of the latter which are discussed on pp. 47-96 below, the action of the humanists in Portugal was mainly devoted to the following tasks : publication of classical Latin dictionaries and grammars; philological commentaries and critical editions of Latin texts; the lexical and syntactical latinization of Portuguese; the revival of Roman law; the use of Latin and very occasionally of Greek in dialogues, letters, apologetical or panegyrical works, bucolic poetry, etc.

Humanists at the court of King John III included at one time or another some remarkable blue-stockings, several of whom were associated with the Infanta Dona Maria (1521-77). She was the scholarly daughter of King Manuel and his third wife, Leonor (sister of Charles V), and she was a fluent Latinist in her own right. These erudite ladies included Joana Vaz (born *c.* 1500) fluent in Latin, Greek, and Hebrew, who surprised Clenardus and Pope Paul III with the elegance of her Latin epistles. Two remarkable sisters of Franco-Spanish origin, Luísa and Angela Sigéa, were both accomplished musicians and linguists. Luísa was an infant prodigy when she came to Portugal in 1543 at the age of twelve or thirteen. By the time she died in childbirth (13 October 1560), she knew Greek, Hebrew, Syriac and Arabic in addition to Latin—a linguistic range of which very few men could boast. Her younger sister, who was even more musical, could only claim a mastery of Greek, Latin and Hebrew; but a good knowledge of these three "divine tongues", spoken by Christ upon the Cross, was enough for her to rate as a fully fledged humanist. Although not a member of the inner Court circle, Publia Hortensia de Castro (1548-1595) was an accomplished Latinist by the age of seventeen. She later astonished King Philip (I of Portugal and II of Castile) with a theological dissertation which she gave before him. She was alleged to have studied at Coimbra University, dressed in boy's clothes and chaperoned by her brother; but in actual fact she probably never left her native province of Alentejo, although her renown reached as far as Rome. Then there was Paula Vicente (born 1513), the musical daughter of dramatist-poet, Gil Vicente (*c.* 1465-*c.*1537).[5] It may be recalled that he was patronised by two Portuguese queens of Spanish origin, Dona Leonor (1458-1525) and Dona Catarina (1507-78), as well as by their respective consorts. Other members of the royal family, whether male or female, received a good classical education at this period, including the *Infante* Dom Luís (1506-1555). who was the most intelligent of all King Manuel's sons.

Even if we do not share Carolina Michaëlis de Vasconcellos' charming historical fantasy that in June 1535 a group of Portuguese and foreign humanists, including Nicholas Clenardus, André de Resende and João de Barros, could have been seen talking animatedly with each other, "and assuredly (with) our Gil Vicente" in the courtyard of the palace at Evora[6], it is undeniable that Barros' upbringing at the court, and his subsequent long and close connection with it, was of greater intellectual advantage to him than a purely university education in Portugal would have been. As indicated above (p. 14), the status and prestige of Portugal's sole university had never been very high. In the first quarter of the sixteenth century it still lagged a long way behind the major foreign universities, as André de Resende explicitly recognized in his *Oratio pro rostris* of 1534, while enumerating at the same time a number of learned men that it had produced since its original foundation in 1290. For various reasons, during the Middle Ages, it functioned at intervals in Coimbra; but after being transferred back to Lisbon in 1377-78, the faculty requested and received a categorical promise from the Crown that it would never be moved again (3 October 1434). In point of fact, King Manuel, dissatisfied with its mediocre standards and teaching, contemplated its removal or drastic overhaul, although nothing concrete was done until the reign of his successor.

From the day of his coronation, John III and the university were not on good terms, and by 1531 the king had definitely decided on its removal and reorganization. He thought at first of moving it to Torres Vedras, but dropped the idea when the municipal council of that little town pleaded abject poverty and the inability to support it. He then decreed its removal to Coimbra, which was effected in December 1536-March 1537, despite the protests of the Rector and Faculty, many of whom were dropped. Its first decade in Coimbra did not bring any drastic improvement either; but this betterment was finally achieved in 1547, with the foundation of the Royal College of Arts, attendance at which was made obligatory for students of several of the courses which were offered at the university proper.

Before the transference of the university from Lisbon to Coimbra, King John III had asked Erasmus to come and teach in Portugal. The latter, who was then at the height of his renown as a classical scholar, religious reformer and social critic, declined on the plea of ill-health and old age. These afflictions were certainly relevant factors; but perhaps a more decisive one was that the Rotterdam-born genius despised and disliked the Portuguese as "a race of Jews".[7] He had previously severely criticised the efforts of the Portuguese Crown to benefit from its Oriental spice-monopoly by maintaining high sale-prices in Europe. However that may have been, King John III's choice for directing the Royal College of Arts at Coimbra was the innovating and enterprising André de Gouveia, called by Montaigne "incomparably the greatest Principal of France" (*sans comparison le plus grand Principal de France*).

André de Gouveia recruited an international faculty of outstanding professors of grammar, rhetoric, poetry, Latin, Greek, Hebrew, logic, philosophy, and mathematics. They included the Scot, George Buchanan, the Frenchman Nicholas Grouchy, and the Portuguese, Diogo de Teive (*c.* 1513-*c.*1565) and João da Costa (1512-78). A brilliant start was made in February 1548, with the inaugural courses being attended by many scions of the nobility. Unfortunately, André de Gouveia died four months later; and several of the others, including George Buchanan, João da Costa and Diogo de Teive, were arrested by the Inquisition and interrogated on suspicion of heretical activities in 1550. They received relatively kid-glove treatment from the Inquisitors, being released after serving short terms of imprisonment or of monastic seclusion.[8] Diogo de Teive was even appointed Principal of the College of Arts in 1552; but the faculty had become demoralised, and the College was handed over to the Jesuits to run on their own more orthodox lines in September 1555. George Buchanan, whose pen was apt to be dipped in gall at the best of times, revenged himself for his very mild imprisonment by writing satirical Latin verses against John III and the Portuguese, once he was safely out of the country.

When the university was reorganized at Coimbra in 1537, the five main faculties of Theology, Canon Law, Civil Law, Medicine, and Arts (including grammar, rhetoric and mathematics) were retained; but the number of courses was increased and some improvements were made in the curriculum. Academically and intellectually, however, the renovated university at Coimbra continued to be, by and large, a stronghold of neo-scholasticism and of obscurantism.

It was also brought under closer control of the Crown. The Rector was no longer elected, but was appointed by the king. The university's grip on high education was strengthened when the maintenance of the *bolseiros del Rei* at foreign universities declined sharply after 1550, and was dropped altogether after the death of King John III.

The spiritual, cultural, and material influence of the Church was always strong and in some ways all-pervasive in this devoutly Roman Catholic country, which for extensive periods of its history can be characterized as being the most priest-ridden in Europe—although not during the reign of King Manuel when João de Barros was being brought up at the court. Criticism of the clergy was never wholly absent, of course. There is a strong strain of anti-clericalism in some of the plays of Gil Vicente, where ignorant or lascivious friars are held up to ridicule, and where wordly or simoniacal prelates (Popes not excepted) are scathingly criticised.[9] But these criticisms of clerical misconduct, like those which we find in the *Ropica Pnefma* (pp. 47-60 below) never impugned the dogmas of the Faith. Anti-clericalism in Portugal never attained (before the nineteenth century) a strength comparable to that in some other Roman Catholic countries, such as France and Italy, or even in Spain. A Protestant movement never developed there, nor did the Northern heresies affect more than a very few maverick individuals. The only real danger to the faith, and the extent of this danger may well have been greatly exaggerated, was that posed by the numerous forcibly converted Jews in 1497, and by their still more numerous descendants, the *Cristãos Novos* or "New Christians".

Both Manuel I and John III were genuinely desirous of reforming the Church in Portugal; and for that matter they kept pressing the Roman Curia to mend its ways. But, at the same time, they set a bad example by securing from a complaisant Papacy bishoprics and other rich ecclesiastical benefices for princes of the blood and for members of the higher nobility, who were often mere children and sometimes infants in arms. For instance, the Infante Dom Afonso was only nine years old and already Bishop of Guarda, when John

III secured for him the wealthy abbey of Alcobaça *in commenda.*

The intellectual formation of many of the secular clergy was rudimentary, and seminaries for training them did not exist until the end of the Council of Trent (1563). The aspiring priest was sometimes educated by an ignorant parish priest who himself knew little more than the rudiments of Latin, and who was barely able to stumble through the Mass and to administer the sacraments. Many of those who were better qualified often received only a meagre benefice, which hardly enabled them to live on the edge of the poverty-line. On the other hand, many of the best benefices were enjoyed by absentee commendators, clerical and lay. Bishops were even accused—apparently with reason—of ordaining individuals who were quite illiterate and who had never been formally examined. Clerical concubinage, almost universal in the Late Middle Ages, was still widespread in the first-half of the sixteenth century. Two Portuguese bishops met by a visiting French Cistercian abbot in 1532, had bestowed some of the best benefices in their respective dioceses on their illegitimate children.[10] The outward forms of religion, however, were often celebrated with great pomp and splendour, mingled with popular enthusiasm and devotion. The sacerdotal and sacro-magical aspects of religion were universally venerated, and there was general agreement with the proverbial saying : "The worst priest is better than the best layman".

The religion of the great bulk of the peasantry can be described as "folk-Catholicism", with pre-Christian beliefs and practices still strongly embedded therein. Two Jesuits observed in 1545 that the country people of Beira needed elementary religious instruction almost as much as did the newly-arrived Negro slaves from Guinea. Other Jesuits record much the same state of affairs all over rural Portugal in the years 1545-1550.[11] The Archbishop of Braga, after visiting the rural districts of his Northern diocese in 1553 lamented "the harm caused by the ignorance of the greater part of the clergy". Seven years later his successor, the saintly Fr. Bartolomeu dos Mártires, complained that "after visiting personally a great part of our archbishopric, we found, apart from what we had been told previously, that there was a great want of qualified persons to preach the word of God and the catechism, both among the clergy and the laity", especially in mountainous Trás-os-Montes.

Nevertheless, it is equally true that the better educated section of the clergy made a valuable contribution to the education of the upper classes. Among the few Portuguese ecclesiastical establishments which elicited glowing—and well deserved—tributes from visiting foreign clergy in the first-half of the sixteenth century was that of the Augustinian Regular Canons at Santa Cruz de Coimbra. Here, Greek, Latin, and Hebrew were taught at a very high level by a Faculty which included a cousin of João de Barros, named Fr. Braz de Barros (also called "of Braga") , between 1527 and 1544. Other religious establishments likewise maintained monastic and cathedral schools, primarily for educating students for the priesthood, but sometimes teaching laymen as well. The Dominican monastery of Benfica at Lisbon had a well deserved reputation for educating boys who included some from the royal household; but the major advance in the sphere of education was due to the Jesuits. The pioneer members of the Society of Jesus reached Portugal in 1540, and they quickly obtained an overwhelming influence at the court, in the towns and in the countryside, which was an established fact by the time that João de Barros died in 1570. Their schools and colleges attracted the best and brightest boys from all social classes, and they often secured the cream of the educational crop for the Society.

Roughly coincident with the arrival and the spectacular success of the Jesuits, was the establishment and development of the Portuguese branch of the Inquisition. During the first decade of his rule, King John III had gradually become convinced that the New Christians constituted a real threat to Roman Catholic orthodoxy—whereas if they had been left alone, it is likely that they would all have become assimilated (or would have emigrated) within two or three generations, as the majority did in any event. At the king's insistence, and after much hesitation on the part of a reluctant Holy See, and some singularly sordid backstairs intrigue at Rome, the Inquisition was introduced in 1536. Its first activities were relatively mild, partly because the Papacy had placed restrictions on its freedom of action, and partly because the first Inquisitor-General, Dom Frei Diogo da Silva, Bishop of Ceuta, was no violent persecutor. Only after his removal and substitution by the *Infante* (later Cardinal) Dom Henrique in 1539 did things get tougher, and the first victims were burnt at Evora in 1543.

Four years later, the Papacy lifted its restrictions on the operation of the Inquisition in Portugal and a preliminary list of prohibited books was compiled. This list, which circulated only in manuscript, included some (but by no means all) of Erasmus' works and some of those of the Spanish Erasmists. In 1551, another and much more comprehensive list of prohibited books was printed and published, placing Portugal in the forefront of the fight against Protestant heresies. This list of 1551 has been described, no doubt correctly, as the most comprehensive and the least liberal of any list of prohibited books published in any Roman Catholic country up till then. It also gave the Portuguese branch of the Inquisition a primacy in censorship which it never lost until its drastic reformation by the Marquis of Pombal over two centuries later. During that period it remained the most obscurantist and the most hidebound of any branch of the Roman Catholic Church. During the last quarter of the sixteenth century the triple literary censorship of the Inquisition, the Ordinary (Episcopal), and the civil *Desembargo do Paço* was increasingly tightened up, making publication a tedious—and often a hazardous—business alike for author, publisher and printer.[12]

Even before the censorship got into its stride by 1550, book production in Portugal was not impressive when compared with that in other West European countries. Printing was a late and a slow starter in "the garden of Europe, planted by the seaside" (*jardim de Europa, à beira-mar plantado*). Apart from a short-lived Jewish press (1487-95), a Portuguese press was mounted at Braga in 1494, through German initiative. A Portuguese printer, Rodrigo Alvares, is recorded in 1497, but German, French and Italian printers continued to control a significant part of the printing business during the first-half of the 16th century. During the whole of this century only about fifty printers working in Portugal, whereas there were over 127 printers working in Lyons alone during the last quarter of the same century. Lisbon, one of the largest cities in Europe and an international entrepot for the colonial trade in 1551, could only boast of having five printers in that year. This number had increased to six by 1567, but it had dropped to four by 1631. There were many more printers at smaller cities in neighbouring Spain, including Barcelona, Seville, Salamanca, and Valencia.

Only some 1,312 editions were printed in Portugal between 1500 and 1600, over half of them at Lisbon. This gives an annual average production of thirteen books, none at all being printed in some years. This makes a sorry showing in comparison with Italy, where there was an annual average of over 113 editions, even allowing for the greater size of the Italian Peninsula. Admittedly, manuscript books also circulated widely, and printed books by Portuguese humanists were often published abroad. But neither in quantity nor in quality did the production of books in Portugal itself come anywhere near what poured from the presses in Spain, France, Flanders, Germany and Italy. Most of the books that were published dealt with religion and theology, but there were five editions of the Manueline *Ordenações*, or code of laws, between 1512 and 1565. It is against this cultural background that the life and work of João de Barros must be considered.[13]

João de Barros was born, in all probability, at Viseu, the capital of Beira Alta, in or about the year 1496. He was of illegitimate birth, his father, Lopo de Barros, being a country gentleman, a citizen of Viseu, a squire (*escudeiro*) of the royal household and the holder of various judicial posts, including that of *corregedor* (magistrate) of the district of Entre Tejo e Odiana. Nothing whatever is known of his mother's status. He was taken into the service of the royal household while still a child, "at the age of spinning tops", to use his own picturesque expression, about the same time that his father died. As mentioned above, he received a much better education at the court from Portuguese and foreign humanists than he could have done at Lisbon University. There is no reason to doubt Severim de Faria's assertion that he was a diligent student of "Latin and Greek, and mathematical sciences and humane letters" (*aprendeo a lingua latina, e grega, e as sciencias Mathematicas, e letras humanas com grande perfeição*), although it is unlikely that his Greek was as good as Severim de Faria claimed. The same authority asserted that his favourite classical authors were Virgil, Lucan, Salust and Livy.[14]

His post in the royal household was that of page of the wardrobe (*moço da guarda-roupa*) to the heir apparent, the *Infante* Dom João, future King John III, who was some six years younger than himself. In 1520, he attracted the attention of King Manuel by writing a precocious chivalresque romance, a genre which was still very popular. Entitled *Chronicle of the Emperor Clarimundo*, it is discussed in the next chapter. The verve and style which he displayed in this lengthy work—written in the space of a few months, so he claimed—induced the King to encourage him in his idea of writing an epic history of the Portuguese in Asia. King Manuel died in December of the following year ; but his successor continued his patronage of the former page of the wardrobe, who now embarked on an official career.

Severim de Faria states that João de Barros was appointed captain and governor of the Castle of Saint George of the Mine (São Jorge da Mina), the Portuguese stronghold on the Gold Coast of Guinea, in 1522, and that he remained there for three years. This assertion seems to be mistaken. Barros is not listed as holding this very important and responsible post in any surviving contemporary or contemporaneous document. Moreover, it is very unlikely that it would have been given to so young and inexperienced a man.[15] On the other hand, Barros himself categorically asserts (*Decade III*, Book 3, chapter 1) that the sailors of a ship in which he was once sailing to Mina (*indo eu para São Jorge da Mina*) caught a swordfish after a hard struggle with it. He does not state exactly when this happened, nor in what capacity he was voyaging to Mina, nor how long he stayed there. It seems likely that he was sent on a visit of inspection, or on some brief official mission, rather than as a captain or governor for three years. However that may have been, this voyage to Guinea was apparently the only occasion on which he ever left Portugal. As it occurred "a few years after 1518", according to his own account, it may well have been in 1522, as Severim de Faria states.

Years later, when writing his *Decade III* in 1539, Barros extolled the courage and loyalty of the African slaves from Guinea, urging his countrymen to employ them on the scale that the Moors of Barbary did, since their military potential was superior to that of the famous Swiss mercenaries in Europe. "And they are so brave that with them we have conquered the other regions which we hold and which do not produce the like". True enough, as the later history of the Portuguese empire showed, in places as far apart as Pernambuco, Ormuz, Ceylon and Macao.[16]

Whatever the nature of the post which Barros held at Mina, this was the beginning of a busy and distinguished bureaucratic career. In 1525-28, he served simultaneously as Treasurer of the three "Houses" or administrative departments of India, Mina, and Ceuta, although he only received the salary for the first-named (*Tesoureiro do dinheiro da Casa da India*, *Tesoureiro da Casa da Mina*, *Tesoureiro-môr da Casa de Ceuta*). It is typical of the niggling formalities (*trâmites*) of the colonial administration that the final closure of his accounts for this period was only officially authorised on the 20 October 1563. Some ten years earlier he was sued by a disgruntled sailor for wages allegedly due to him from that period; but Barros explained that he could not possibly recall after a lapse of twenty-seven years whether this particular payment had been made, as during his term of office he had paid "some ten or twelve thousand mariners".

For reasons still uncertain, his bureaucratic career was temporarily interrupted in 1530-32, when he retired to live at his *quinta*, or country estate, of São Lourenço do Ribeiro de Alitem (or Litem) near Pombal. It was here, "in this solitary place where plague, earthquakes, and heavy winter rains have frustratingly confined me,"[17] that he composed in 1531 the treatise entitled *Ropica Pnefma* (*Spiritual Merchandise*), which is discussed in chapter 3. This property was part of the dowry of his wife, Maria de Almeida, daughter of a colleague in the royal bureaucracy. Barros was clearly very attached to this place, since he greatly enlarged and improved the estate over the years by buying up adjoining lands and building a hermitage with a chapel dedicated to Santo António. He likewise bought and sold properties at Lisbon to improve his house there, and may have over-reached himself in so doing. His previously quoted reference to earthquakes is an allusion to the severe series of shocks which were felt throughout Portugal in January 1531. Lisbon suffered very heavy damage to buildings and great loss of life, the king and many of the inhabitants having to camp out in the fields.

João de Barros evidently returned to Lisbon some time in 1532, since his letter of appointment as Factor of the India and Guinea Houses (*Feitor das Casas da Guiné e India*) dated 25 December 1533, states that he had already been exercising this post since the retirement of his predecessor in the previous year. Thenceforward, until his own retirement in August 1567, he led a double life, combining the career of an active and conscientious bureaucrat with that of a busy and didactic writer. As he himself wrote in the prologue addressed to the king in his first *Decade* (1552) : "Your Highness likewise soon appointed me Treasurer of the Houses of India and Mina, and subsequently as Factor of the said Houses—burdensome charges, which with their weight bow down a man's life, since they are full-time positions, and, with their daily press of business concerning shipping and trade, they suffocate and repress any liberal spirit. But it seems that such was ordained for me from above, so that not only should I be fated to cope with the chores of administering the trades of Africa and Asia, but also to record the exploits which your vassals performed in the warfare and conquest thereof".[18] In order to satisfy both claims on his time, Barros tells the king in the same prologue : "I divided my lifetime by devoting the days to my official work, and a part of the nights to this writing of your *Asia* ; and in this way I fulfilled both the regulations of the office and the desire which I always had of undertaking this literary enterprise."

The official office-hours on working days, as laid down in King Manuel's *Regimento*, or regulations for the India and Guinea Houses promulgated in 1509, were : 6–10 a.m. and 3–6 p.m. in Summer, and 8–11 a.m. and 2–5 p.m. in Winter. However, it was stipulated that if pressure of business so required, then the officials were to work "a little longer". Doubtless Barros' put in much unpaid overtime when ships were arriving or being dispatched in considerable numbers. He was the Factor of both Houses, although their respective staffs were separately organized.[19]

It is clear from incidental references in the *Decades* that João de Barros was intermittently engaged on writing them since the time that he had published *Clarimundo*. It is equally clear that the first three, and perhaps the fourth, had been completed in draft form by 1539. But he had other irons in the fire besides *Clarimundo* and *Ropica Pnefma*. He delivered an Erasmian-style panegyric to King John III at Evora in 1533, and another, with less pronounced but still recognizable Erasmian overtones, to the erudite Infanta Dona Maria in 1545. These are discussed in chapter 4. More importantly, between 1539 and 1545, Barros composed a remarkable series of didactic and pedagogical works, the majority of which were published in 1539-40, and which are discussed in chapter 5. After 1545, he seems to have concentrated on retouching and polishing the drafts of his *Decades* for publication, and on gathering material for other geographic, economic, and even architectural works, which, in the event, never saw the light of day, as explained in chapter 7.

King John III evidently appreciated the bureaucratic, didactic, and historical labours of his erstwhile page, since he made him numerous monetary and other grants between 1521 and 1557. Unfortunately for Barros, the substantial sums which he received from these and other sources did not cover his expenditure in the long run. Apart from his extensive property dealings in town and country, in which he may well have over-extended himself, he speculated heavily and disastrously in the colonisation of Brazil.

Francisco Pizarro's conquest of the Inca empire in 1530-32, and the spectacular amounts of gold and silver treasure which it yielded, had convinced many Portuguese that rich gold and silver mines must be awaiting discovery and exploitation in the hinterland of the sparsely settled Brazilian coastline. At the same time, the growing menace that the French might settle permanently in this portion of South America, which had been assigned to the Portuguese Crown by the outcome of the Treaty of Tordesillas (1494), induced King John III systematically to promote the colonisation of Brazil. The system which he adopted in 1534 was to divide the coastline between the Amazon river and São Vicente into a dozen hereditary captaincies (*capitanias*) of a limited width but with an indefinite extension into the interior. Each captaincy was placed under a *donatário*, or lord-proprietor, with extensive rights and privileges, João de Barros being among the earliest grantees.[20] In association with Aires da Cunha and Alvares de Andrade, he sent an expedition of some 900 men, including 113 horsemen, in nine or ten ships to colonise and to search for gold in the region of the Maranhão (N.E. Brazil). As he later observed, this expedition included the greatest number of mounted men who had ever been sent to such a great distance from Portugal.[21] It was certainly more than either Cortes or Pizarro commanded when they launched their respective invasions of the Aztec and the Inca empires. Not surprisingly the Spanish envoy at Lisbon tried to find out what he could about this expedition, despite the secrecy which shrouded it.

Unfortunately, most of the ships carrying this expedition were shipwrecked on arrival, and after three years of unsuccessful efforts the survivors gave up the struggle and got away in three caravels to the Antilles. Despite this catastrophe, João de Barros sent another expedition to the same region in 1556, this time accompanied by two of his sons, Jerónimo (the eldest) and João. They struggled vainly for five years against hostile natives and the unfamiliar climate and ecology ; but the few survivors in their turn either returned to Portugal or else moved to more promising regions in Brazil. This double fiasco landed João de Barros in pecuniary difficulties for the rest of his life ; partly because in addition to losing all the capital which he had invested in these-disastrous expeditions, he undertook to pay pensions to the widows and orphans of the first one.[22]

João de Barros' personal interest in the colonisation of Brazil is evidenced not only by the two costly expeditions which he organized, and by occasional references in his *Decades*, but by a curious passage in Richard Hakluyt's *Divers Voyages* first published at London in 1582. In the "Epistle dedicatory" of this little work, addressed to "the most virtuous Gentleman master Philip Sydney Esquire",[23] Hakluyt urges the advisability of the English colonising North America with the help of able-bodied jail-birds, "which for small robberies are daily hanged up in great numbers, even twenty at a clap out of one jaii (as was seen at the last assizes in Rochester)". Invoking the Portuguese precedent in this respect, Hakluyt continues: "It chanced very lately that upon occasion I had great conference in matters of cosmography with an excellent learned man of Portingale, most privy to all the discoveries of his nation, who wondered that those blessed countries from the point of Florida northward, were all this while unplanted by Christians, protesting with great affection and zeal, that if he were now as young as I (for at this present he is three score years of age) he would sell all he had, being a man of no small wealth and honour, to furnish a convenient number of ships to sea for the inhabiting of those countries, and reducing those gentile people to Christianity. Moreover he added that John Barros, their chief cosmographer, being moved with the like desire, was the cause that Brasilia was first inhabited by the Portingales : where they have nine baronies or lordships (*capitanias*) and thirty engennies (*engenhos*) or sugar-mills, two or three hundred slaves belonging to each mill, with a judge, and other officers, and a church : so that every mill is as it were a little commonwealth: and that the country was first planted by such men, as for small offences were saved from the rope. This he spoke not only unto me and in my hearing, but also in the presence of a friend of mine, a man of great skill in the mathematics".[24]

Elsewhere Hakluyt tells us that his informant was António de Castilho, late Portuguese envoy at London and keeper of the archives at Lisbon. He also has two marginal notes : "the speech of a learned Portingale", and "Master John Barros the cause of the inhabiting of Brasilia". There seems no reason to doubt the honesty and reliability of the "excellent learned man of Portingale, of singular gravity, authority and experience", as Hakluyt describes António de Castilho elsewhere, although Barros was never "chief cosmographer" (*cosmografo-mór*) of Portugal, but a recognized expert and writer on this science. Nor was Barros the sole advocate of the systematic colonisation of Brazil, but he was evidently one of the most persistent and influential.[25] His advice would in all probability have weighed heavily with King John III, even if his own efforts to practice what he preached had backfired so disastrously.

From the foregoing, and from the consideration of his voluminous literary output, it is clear that João de Barros was essentially a man who scorned delights to live laborious days. The thirty-four years which he spent as Factor of the India and Guinea Houses were enough to age anyone prematurely, as he himself claimed. In this very responsible post, he had to oversee, in whole or in part, the organization and dispatch of shipping to India, Africa and Brazil; to arrange for the receipt, storage, and distribution of the most varied return-cargoes, including spices, slaves, diamonds, porcelain, brazil-wood, silk and cotton textiles, etcetera, etcetera; to receive and register all incoming correspondence, and all outgoing official correspondence; to maintain an archive and records; and to coordinate a complex interlocking and overlapping system of finance and administration. In addition to these onerous official responsibilities, which inevitably increased with the expansion of the Portuguese seaborne empire during his term of office, he had to cope with mounting personal indebtedness from 1535 onwards, and with a growing family, which eventually included ten children (five boys and five girls).[26]

Under such varied and mounting pressures, and although it is obvious that his wife must have been a true helpmate, it is hardly surprising that João de Barros was incapacitated by a stroke, which forced his retirement from office to his beloved *quinta* of São Lourenço de Alitem in August 1567. Even then, he did not apparently give up hope of completing some of his unpublished works, as a Jesuit friend reported in a letter dated February 1569.[27] But he had driven himself too hard for too long. Another stroke proved fatal to him on the 21 October 1570, when he died paralysed and speechless (*entrevado, sem falar, de ar de apoplexia*), according to an eyewitness.

In the autograph (undated) draft of his last will and testament he declared : "I have many debts, which are known to my wife and children, in whose company and for whose maintenance, I incurred them all. Or rather, speaking more accurately, they were really incurred in the service of our lord the king". He added that he hoped that his unpublished works would be printed and presented to the king, "for whom the results of my labours were always intended".[28] On his retirement in 1567, the Crown had written off all the money which he still owed for artillery and materials supplied for his expeditions to the Maranhão. Nevertheless, he died so deeply indebted that several of his heirs renounced their shares of the bankrupt estate in 1577. His widow, fortunately for her, received a pension from the grateful Crown, which, it must be said, whether in the persons of Manuel I, John III, and the Queen-Regent Catherine, was always appreciative of this loyal and hard-working servant. Yet, in 1590, his heirs were being sued for debts still outstanding to the royal exchequer; and in 1603 one of his grandsons was imprisoned for an unpaid debt of João de Barros due to a private creditor.[29]

At his own desire, Barros was buried in the little chapel dedicated to St. Anthony on his country estate. In 1610, his godson, Bishop Dom Jorge de Ataide, exhumed and removed his remains to the parochial church of Alcobaça, intending to rebury them in a sumptuous mausoleum which he designed to build there. Unfortunately, Dom Jorge died before he did so. Hence the exact resting-place of one of Portugal's greatest sons during her golden age is, like those of Gil Vicente and Luís de Camões, uncertain.

João de Barros was described by a Portuguese Jesuit who knew him in 1563 as being : "a man of venerable aspect, fair complexion, with piercing eyes and an aquiline nose, and a flowing white beard; he was of medium height, with a spare frame. He was a fluent and pleasant if serious conversationalist". The accuracy of this description is confirmed by an (undated) engraving, included by Severim de Faria in his *Discursos* of 1624, and which was evidently made from a portrait painted some sixty years earlier.[30]

The significance of his work, and its influence among contemporaries and to posterity, will emerge in the succeeding chapters. Here, it will suffice to recall the claim of his first biographer that if João de Barros had no sumptuous marble tomb to perpetuate his memory, his published works afford a more durable and admirable monument.

NOTES

1. Virginia Rau, "Alguns estudantes e eruditos portugueses em Itália no século XV," in *Do Tempo e da História* (Faculdade de Letras de Lisboa, 1973), 24-99; Joaquim de Carvalho, *Estudos sobre a cultura portuguesa do século XV* (Coimbra, 1949), and *Estudos sobre a cultura portuguesa do século XVI* (2 vols., Coimbra, 1947-48); Marcel Bataillon, *Etudes sur le Portugal au temps de l'humanisme* (Coimbra, 1946); Luis de Matos, *Les Portugais à l'Université de Paris entre 1500 et 1550* (Coimbra, 1950); Joaquim Veríssimo Serrão, *Portugueses no Estudo de Toulouse* (Coimbra, 1954), and *Portugueses no Estudo de Salamanca* (Lisboa, 1962); Antonio José Saraiva, *História da Cultura em Portugal* (3 vols., Lisboa, 1950-62); José Sebastião da Silva Dias, *Correntes de sentimento religioso em Portugál* (Coimbra, 1960); Ibidem, *A politica cultural da época de Dom João III* (Coimbra, 1969); Ibidem *Os Descobrimentos e a problemàtica cultural do século XVI* (Coimbra, 1973). For a brief survey in English see A.H. de Oliveira Marques, *History of Portugal*, I, *From Lusitânia to Empire* (Columbia University Press 1973), pp. 190-207.
2. For the editions of Nicholas von Poppelau see R. Foulché-Delbosc, *Bibliographie de Voyages en Espagne et en Portugal* (Paris, 1896, facsimile reprint by Meridian Publishing Corp., Amsterdam, 1969), P. 19, nr. 13. For Jerome Münzer see Basilio de Vasconcelos (ed. and trans.), *Itinerario do Dr. Jerônimo Münzer. Excertos* (Coimbra, 1931). Both texts available in Spanish translation in J. Garcia Mercadal, *Viajes de Extranjeros por España y Portugal . . . hasta fines del siglo XVI* (Madrid, 1952), pp. 307 ff.
3. *Oração de Sapiencia. Oratio Pro Rostris* (ed. and trans. *A.* Moreira de Sá and Miguel Pinto de Meneses, Lisboa, 1956).
4. M. Gonçalves Cerejeira, *O Renascimento em Portugal. Clenardo e a sociedade portuguesa do seu tempo* (3rd ed., Coimbra, 1949).
5. J.H. Parker, *Gil Vicente* (Twayne Publishers Inc,. 1967)
6. Carolina Michaelis de Vasconcelos, *Notas Vicentinas. Preliminares duma edição critica das obras de Gil Vicente* (ed. Lisboa, 1949), p. 53.
7. M. Bataillon, *Etudes sur le Portugal au temps de l'humanisme* (Coimbra, 1953).
8. Mário Brandão, *A Inquisição e os Professores do Colégio das Artes* (Coimbra, 1948).
9. J.H. Parker, *Gil Vicente* (1967), pp. 85, 92, 94-95.

10. Dom Maur Cocheril (ed.), *Frère Claude de Broneval. Peregrinantio Hispanica : voyage de Dom Esme de Saulieu, Abbé de Clairvaux en l'Espagne et au Portugal, 1531-33* (Paris, 1970).
11. Francisco Rodrigues, S.J. *Historia da Companhia de Jesus na Assistência de Portugal*, Vol. I (1), pp. lvi, 653 (Lisboa, 1931), Vols. I-II (2) of this work cover our period.
12. I.S. Révah, *La Censure Inquisitoriale Portugaise au XVIe siècle. Etude accompagnée de la reproduction en facsimile des Index* (Lisboa, 1960); J.S. da Silva Dias, *O Primeiro Rol de Livros Proibidos* (Coimbra, 1963).
13. António Joaquim Anselmo, *Bibliografia das obras impressas em Portugal no século XVI* (Lisboa, 1926); A.J. Saraiva, *Historia da Cultura em Portugal*, vol. II, pp. 124-41, for the above and what follows.
14. The basic biography of João de Barros is still that by Manuel Severim de Faria, *Discursos varios politicos* (Evora, 1624), fls. 22-61, supplemented by the documents from the Torre do Tombo and elsewhere edited by António Baião, *Documentos inéditos sôbre João de Barros, sobre o escritor seu homónimo contemporãneo, sobre a família do historiador e sôbre os continuadores das suas "Decadas"* (Coimbra, 1917), and in his introduction, pp. v-lxxxii, to the *Asia de Joam de Barros Primeira Decada* (all published) (Coimbra, 1932). Save where otherwise stated, the facts in my biographical sketch are taken from either Severim de Faria or Baião.
15. For the importance of São Jorge da Mina as a source of gold for the Crown of Portugal, 1482-1637, and more particularly during the first-half of the sixteenth-century, see Vitorino Magalhães-Godinho, *L'Economie de l'Empire Portugais aux XVe et XVIe siècles* (Paris, 1969), pp. 209-43. A document in the archives of the Royal Mint at Lisbon, gives a João de Barros as commander of the caravel *Nazaré*, which returned from Mina in October 1521 (*op. cit.*, p. 230). but this could be a homonym. For the original castle and the subsequent Dutch alterations, see A.W. Lawrence, *Trade Castles and Forts of West Africa* (London, 1963), pp. 103-30.
16. *Decada I* Livro 3, cap. xii; C.R. Boxer, *The Portuguese Seaborne Empire* (Pelican ed., 1973), pp. 303-04.
17. ". . . em este ermo onde peste, tremores da terra e grandes invernadas me tinham cercado com enfadamento".
18. We lack a good modern monograph on the complex and interlocking system of the Guinea, India and Ceuta Houses, but some idea of the duties and responsibilities of João de Barros can be obtained from the following : Damião Peres (ed.) *Regimento das Casas da India e Mina* (Coimbra, 1947); C.R. Boxer, "Duas cartas inéditas de João de Barros quando Feitor da Casa da India," in *Congresso Internacional de História dos Descobrimentos* (4-page reprint from the *Actas do Congresso*, Lisboa, 1961); James L. Vogt, "The Lisbon Slave House and the African Trade, 1486-1521," in *Proceedings of*

the American Philosophical Society, Vol. 117 (Philadelphia 1973), pp. 1-16.

19. ". . . reparti o tempo da vida, dando os dias ao ofício e parte das noites a esta escritura da vóssa Asia, e assi compri com o regimento do ofício e com o desejo que sempre tive desta impresa."

20. The full text of the Crown's donation of his captaincy, d. Evora, 8 March 1535, in A. Baião (ed.), *Asia de Joam de Barros*, (Coimbra, 1932), pp. xxviii-xxxiv. For the late medieval origins of these donatary-captaincies, the previous studies of Carlos Malheiro Dias, Alexander Merchant, *et al.*, have been superseded by H.B. Johnson Jr., "The Donatary-Captaincy in perspective : Portuguese backgrounds to the settlement of Brazil," In *Hispanic-American Historical Review*, Vol. 52 (1972), pp. 203-14.

21. " . . . A qual armada foi de novecentos homens em que entrarão cento e treze de cavallo, cousa que para tão longe nunca sayo deste reino" *Decada I*, Livro 6, Cap. 1).

22. Severim de Faria (*Discursos*, 1624, fls. 30-32) has confused the two expeditions of 1539 and 1556, telescoping them into one. For the Spanish envoy's interest and reports see V. Magalhães Godinho, *L'Economie de l'Empire Portugais* (Paris, 1969), p. 485.

23. For this renowned Elizabethan soldier, poet and cavalier, see James M. Osborn, *Young Philip Sydney, 1572-77* (Yale University Press, 1972).

24. Richard Hakluyt the Younger, *Divers voyages touching the discoveries of America, and the Islands adjacent unto the same . . . And certaine of advertisements for observations necessaire for such as shall hereafter make the like attempt* (facsimile edition of the 1582 edition by David Quinn, Amsterdam, 1967), pp. (5)-(6); E. G. R. Taylor (ed.) *The original writings and correspondences of the two Richard Hakluyts* (2 vols., London, 1935), Vol. 1 pp. 23, 176, 376.

25. For example, Diogo de Gouveia Senior, who urged King John III to colonise Brazil with several thousand colonists from the Azores.

26. Jerónimo (served in the Brazil-Maranhão, 1556-61, died, 1586); António (served in Morocco and died in Hungary); João (served in the Brazil-Maranhão, India and Morocco, dying at Leiria in 1578 on his return from Arzila); Diogo (served eight years in India, and killed by Malabar corsairs in 1575); Lopo (served in India, where he married, and died after being captain of Bacaim); Dona Maria; Dona Isabel (married her cousin, Lopo de Barros); Dona Catarina (married Christovão de Mello); Dona Ana (nun); another girl, name unknown.

27. Cipriano Soares, S.J., in a letter d. Coimbra, 22 Feb. 1569, to Diego Miron, S.J., at Rome : "concerning what your Reverence asks about the work of João de Barros, Our Lord was served to allow him to be stricken with a paralysis of the mouth over a year ago. For this reason he was relieved from his office . . . and he is

in an estate of his near Leiria, where he will finish this (work on Japan), and if God grants him life, he will also complete the Maps and Cosmography of the East , which will be the most useful of all the works which he has undertaken" (*apud* G. Schurhammer, S.J., *Gesammelte Studien*, II, *Orientalia* (Rome-Lisbon, 1963), p. 557.

28. Autograph draft for the will of João de Barros, undated, but *circa* 1569/70, *apud* Antonio Baião, *Documentos Inéditos*, pp. 66-69.

29. António Baião, *Documentos Inéditos*, p. 121.

30. ". . . homem de veneravel presença, alvo de cor, olhos espertos, e nariz aquilino, barba comprida, e toda branca, magro, e não grande de corpo, na pratica ainda que grave era aprasivel, e de grande conversação, Foi varão de vida exemplar, e mui pio . . ." (Severim de Faria, *Discursos Varios Politicos*, Evora, 1624, fls. 54-55). His informant was the Jesuit.

2

CHRONICLE OF THE EMPEROR CLARIMUNDO, 1522

As mentioned previously, João de Barros began his literary career with a novel of chivalry, written in the usual pattern for a work of this kind, which was still very popular in the courts and cultured circles of the Iberian peninsula.[1] Entitled *First Part of the Chronicle of the Emperor Clarimundo, from whom the kings of Portugal are descended*, Barros claimed to have written it in the space of eight months, during the year 1520, with the encouragement both of King Manuel and the *Infante* Dom João. It was published two years later, with a double prologue or preface, one addressed to Dom João as *Infante* and the other to him as king. From these and from the prologue to the first *Decade* (1552), we learn that Barros composed this work partly with the idea "of polishing the style of my capacity for this your *Asia*." He read some parts of the manuscript to King Manuel in 1520. The monarch was so pleased with them, that he encouraged Barros to finish the work and gave him a half-promise that he would entrust him in due course with compiling an epic history of the Portuguese in Asia.[2]

In accordance with a convention common to many of these chivalresque novels, the chronicle purported to be translated from an original Hungarian manuscript recounting the adventurous life of the "Emperor" Clarimundo. This fictitious character is here presented as the grandfather of Count Henry of Burgundy, who was the real father of Dom Afonso Henriques, the first king of Portugal and founder of the Burgundian dynasty. Needless to say, this transparent device could not have deceived anyone at the court (nor was it intended to do so), as everyone knew that young Barros did not know a word of Magyar.

The plot, if such it can be termed, was a singularly complicated and labyrinthine one, even for this type of novel, whose prime exemplar was *Amadis of Gaul*, the first known edition of which was published in 1508. There are over 250 characters or personages in the 104 chapters of *Clarimundo*, which is crowded with an inextricable medley of natural, supernatural, magical, and palpably absurd events. Sub-plots abound. Characters appear, disappear and reappear, with bewildering rapidity. Knights battle with each other, with Muslims, and with monsters, time and time again. Giants, wizards, magicians, enchantments, spells and incantations of both black and white magic, jostle each other on nearly every page. The only consistent feature is a tailpiece containing some sententious moral reflexion(s) at the end of each and every chapter. An adequate summary of the meandering plot would run to many pages, and the barest outline must suffice here.

The novel begins with the marriage of King Adrian of Hungary with Briania, daughter of King Claudius of France, and the birth of their son, Clarimundo ("light" or "clarity" of the world). He was so called because of his singular beauty, and because he was born on a beautiful clear dawn after a night of most violent storm and an attack on the capital city by the Turks. Incidentally, this exceptionally stormy night may be an allusion to the birth of John III (6 June 1502) when "there raged the most terrible tempest that any man then living could remember", as a sixteenth-century Englishman wrote. While still in the cradle, Clarimundo was exchanged for a dead baby of the same age, whose mother had accidentally overlaid him in her sleep, and who then fled from the palace with the royal infant. Only long afterwards did the bereaved royal family learn that their son was still alive.

Meanwhile, Clarimundo was found by a disconsolate and childless widow named Dona Grionesa, rather like Moses was found in the bullrushes by Pharaoh's daughter. Not knowing the child's name, she called him Belifonte. He was brought up in an island near Sicily, where he became a daring huntsman and horseman, and very desirous of becoming a knight-errant. A storm brought him to the French coast, and he was subsequently knighted by King Claudius, who had no idea that the singularly handsome young Belifonte was his own grandson. Then begins the long and ever more complicated chain of the adventures and misadventures of Belifonte-Clarimundo. Even after being reunited in chapter 20 with his parents at Buda, he continues in his role as a wandering knight-errant. He is victorious in innumerable fights, battles, and duels, defending the good and the weak, punishing and subduing the wicked, and protecting fair damsels of all kinds. He also assumes other names and titles, including "the knight of the sad tears" (*cavaleiro das lagrimas tristes*) and "the carefree cavalier" (*cavaleiro descuidado*).

In the course of one of his adventures, he saves the life of the Princess Clarinda, daughter of the Emperor of Constantinople or Byzantium. They fall in love with each other, but are periodically separated by a series of untoward events and misunderstandings, inevitable in these romances, where the course of true love never did run smooth. However, they remain faithful to each other, and are eventually reunited in a clandestine marriage. After one of his exploits, Clarimundo meets the Princess Farpinda, who falls in love with him, but he rejects her advances. In revenge, she gives him a potion to drink which makes him lose his memory. Sometime later, a wise man, Fanimor, gives him a miraculous sword, which restores his memory when he girds it on.

The hero and Fanimor then sail to the Rock of Sintra where they disembark, and Clarimundo kills the local giant after a homeric combat. Fanimor then takes Clarimundo up to the top of an exceedingly high tower, whence they have a view of "a great part of the land and of the sea". Fanimor prophesies the advent and rise of Portugal, culminating with the discoveries and conquests of the reign of King Manuel. After further adventures and a gigantic battle with the Turks besieging Constantinople, Clarimundo is again reunited with Clarinda, this time with an official marriage, and her father hands over the government of the empire to his son-in-law. In due time, a son named Sancho is born to the happy couple. When he reaches manhood, he is taken by enchantment in a ship to Spain, where King Alfonso gives him his daughter, Dona Lucinda, in marriage. The nuptial feasting and rejoicing at Toledo are at their height when news is received of the death of Clarimundo. The chronicle ends somewhat abruptly with "Heaven showing how little time pleasures endure without being accompanied by sorrows" (*mostrando o céu quam pouco duram os prazeres sem serem acompanhados dos pezares*).

The sudden and offhand manner in which Clarimundo's death receives a bare mention, after the prolix details devoted to his knightly prowess and virtues, gives the impression that Barros had got bored with his own story and decided to terminate it abruptly. Certainly, he never wrote the second part, despite the implication of the wording of the title to the first edition. In any event, *Clarimundo* proved to be the most popular of all the published works of João de Barros in his own lifetime and for long afterwards, as Severim de Faria rather sourly and sententiously observed in 1624 : "this book being fabulous and the first fruits of his youth, it had better fortune in being reprinted than the other works, including the *Decades*, by the same author. Whence we see how the majority is governed rather by fancy than by reason, and that the good usually appeals only to a minority".[3]

The prolixity of the narrative in *Clarimundo* did not adversely affect the author's prose style, which is devoid of turgidity in this work, though not of sententiousness. Aubrey Bell, an exceptionally well-qualified critic, even though he could rarely bring himself to write an unkind word about any of the Portuguese classics, commented : "The most remarkable feature of this work. . . is its inexhaustible flow of clear, smooth, vigorous prose, entirely free from awkwardness or hesitation".[4] Fair enough ; but the average modern reader is likely to find it very difficult to maintain an interest in the adventures and misadventures of so many cardboard characters.

João de Barros' indebtedness to the famous exemplar of this type of romance, *Amadis of Gaul*, is obvious. This fact has been stressed by Professor Marques Braga in the introduction and notes to his 3-volume edition of *Clarimundo* in the series Clássicos Sá da Costa, to which the interested reader is referred. It is probable that Barros also owed something to a slightly later work by a famous Castilian contemporary, Gonzalo Fernandez de Oviedo y Valdéz

(1478-1557), whose *Claribalte* was printed at Valencia in 1519. This, in its turn, was indebted to previous works in this well-tilled field, including *Tirant lo Blanch*, published in Catalan at Valencia in 1490.

Admittedly, even if João de Barros had read *Claribalte*, as I strongly suspect, his indebtedness to this work was not great. *Claribalte* is not nearly so fantastic as *Clarimundo*, and it is not nearly so long. There is much less of the supernatural, and the plot is uncomplicated and easy to follow in the book's eighty-two chapters. It purports to be translated with the help of a Tartar(!) from an original manuscript acquired in the kingdom of "Phirolt"; but the action occurs mainly in England, where the hero becomes enamoured of the Crown Princess. As with *Clarimundo*, there are two marriages, one clandestine (ch. 23) and the other public and official (chs. 72-74). Although Oviedo wrote the work when he was in the West Indies, holding a post as comptroller of the gold mines in Hispaniola, the action is confined to Europe. There is no mention of Castile's colonial expansion to parallel Fanimor's prophecy of Portuguese expansion in *Clarimundo*.

We may recall that Oviedo, the famous *conquistador*-chronicler, later became a severe critic of these romances of chivalry, including by implication his own *Claribalte*. In 1535, in his *General History of the Indies* (*La Historia Natural y General de las Indias*), Book 6, chapter viii, Oviedo reminds his readers that he is not "telling them nonsense like the lying books of *Amadis* and those which depend on them".[5] Barros, on the other hand, seems to have had no misgivings in later years about his *Clarimundo*. He records complacently in the preface to his *Ropica Pnefma* that his relative, colleague and friend, Duarte de Resende, had read it with pleasure and profit in the distant Moluccan island of Ternate, "whence merchants bring their spicy drugs" (*pace* Milton). He also puts in a word in favour of these chivalresque romances in his panegyric to King John III delivered in 1533.

Despite Fernandez de Oviedo's denunciation of the novels of chivalry, and however much the twentieth-century reader may be inclined to agree with him, there is no doubt but that this genre remained popular with Iberian readers throughout the sixteenth century. Menendez y Pelayo and other modern critics have claimed that these fantastic romances could not hold their own against the veracious chronicles of Iberian exploits in America, Asia and Africa, or on the battlefields of Italy, Flanders, and Germany.[6] In fact, however, the two co-existed quite happily for generations, and many veteran *conquistadores* were ardent readers of *Amadis* and its successors ; even if Oviedo was not among them after the conquest of Mexico had shown that truth could be stranger than fiction. If Fr. Amador Arrais (15??-1600), a Carmelite friar who became Bishop of Portalegre, adversely criticised *Clarimundo* and other romances of this type in his *Diálogos* (1589, 1604), they were warmly defended as late as 1619 by Francisco Rodrigues Lobo in his *Corte na Aldea e Noites do Inverno* (*Court in the Village on Winter Nights*). He gave instances from real life (so he said) of men having been inspired to do doughty deeds, and damsels strengthened in guarding their virginity, by their perusal of such books.[7]

These romances of chivalry can in a way be considered as the sixteenth-century equivalents of the present-day novels of "sex n' violence". But the sex in the former genre is invariably sublimated, and the violence very seldom has sadistic overtones, being mostly of the Shakespearian variety : "lay on Macduff, and damned be him that first cries 'hold, enough'." The first passage in *Clarimundo* which may infer any sexual union between the hero and Clarinda is on the night of their clandestine marriage (Book II, ch. 32) ; but even this scene is so obscurely worded that they may have done nothing more than kiss each other repeatedly.

Nevertheless, prudish clerical moralists often denounced these books as conducive to immoral thoughts. Jesuit missionaries on board Portuguese Indiamen bound for "Golden Goa" made a practice of seizing such "pernicious works", which they found passengers reading. They threw the offending books overboard, and gave their readers devotional works and religious tracts in exchange. The passengers were not always pleased with the end-results of this forcible exchange, although the Jesuits professed to believe that they were.[8] But the correspondence of the Goa inquisitors with their headquarters at Lisbon shows us that in fact their popularity continued unabated.[9]

All commentators agree that for modern readers the most interesting and significant portion of *Clarimundo* is the prophecy of Fanimor concerning Portuguese expansion overseas (Book III, ch. 4). It is a fairly safe bet that this chapter must have been one of the portions which Barros read to King Manuel from the original manuscript in 1520, and which gave that monarch the idea that the aspiring young author might become the man to write the history of the Portuguese exploits in the East. Fanimor's prophecy, which is partly in prose and partly in *ottava rima*, has obvious affinities with the famous *Lusíadas* of Luís de Camões (1572). This applies especially to canto II, stanzas 44-55, of the epic poem, although whether Camões actually derived his inspiration from reading this portion of *Clarimundo* must remain an open question. The most that can be said is that he could easily have done so, and many competent critics are convinced that he did.[10]

As with the *Lusíadas*, Fanimor's prophecy in *Clarimundo* gives a summary of Portuguese history, beginning with Count Henry of Burgundy and King Dom Afonso Henriques. Both poems describe the legendary defeat of the five Moorish kings in the battle of Ourique, with the granting of the escutcheon of the *quinas* and the divine guarantee of Portugal's future greatness as an empire. Portuguese participation in the decisive victory of the Salado is treated in similar fashion in both poems; but Barros omits all mention of the tragic death of Inês de Castro, which inspired some of Camões' most famous lines. Both Barros and Camões extol King John I and the victory over the Castilians at Aljubarrota on "Saint Mary of August" (14 August 1385), as also the Portuguese conquests in Morocco, including the capture of Alcacer Seguir and Arzila.

Both poems celebrate in very similar terms the expansion of the Faith and of Empire to the uttermost ends of the earth.[11] The gold of Sofala and the Island of St. Lawrence feature equally in both. As in the *Luísadas*, Fanimor in *Clarimundo* surveys "Portuguese Asia" and Portuguese exploits therein, from the Cape of Good Hope to China and the Ryukyus. If Camões goes a little further and ends up in Japan, this was because the island-empire had not yet been discovered by the Portuguese when Barros wrote. Barros, like Camões, and for that matter like Milton, was clearly fascinated by the sound of exotic Asian place-names, liberally sprinkling his lines with them.[12] His muse is, admittedly, more flat-footed than that of Camões, and his verses are interlarded with passages of descriptive prose. But the resemblances between this portion of *Clarimundo* and the *Lusíadas* are indeed striking, and they are there for all to see.

Before taking leave of *Clarimundo*, we may note that just as Barros borrowed freely from his predecessors, so he was laid under contribution by his successors, even if we do not count Camões among these. Francisco de Moraes (1500-1572), author of *Palmeirim de Inglaterra* (*Palmeirim of England*), knew Barros personally. As several critics have pointed out, he borrowed freely from *Clarimundo* in his own romance, which was apparently first published in 1544. although the oldest surviving edition is dated 1567, Other Portuguese editions of *Palmeirim* followed in 1592, 1786 and 1852. Unlike *Clarimundo*, which found no foreign translator, *Palmeirim* had a great (indeed, an astonishing) success abroad. No fewer than eight editions were published in Italy between 1553 and 1609, and there were four English editions between 1602 and 1664.[13]

NOTES

1. Henry Thomas, *Spanish and Portuguese Romances of Chivalry* (Cambridge University Press, 1920); Irving A. Leonard, *Books of the Brave* (Harvard University Press, 1949).
2. ". . . dizendo aver dias que desejáva estas cousas das pártes do oriente serem póstas em escriptura, mas que nunca achára pessoa de que ò confiasse, que se me eu atrevia a esta obra (como o debuxo mostráva) o meu trabalho nam seria antelle perdido" (*Decada I, prologo*)
3. *Discursos* (1624), fls. 38-39. The only recorded copy is that in the National Library of Madrid, of which Professor Eugenio Asensio kindly showed me a photographic copy in October, 1973. A second edition was published in 1555, which is nearly as rare, and of which I saw the fine copy in the late King Manuel II's library at Vila Viçosa in November 1973. This copy is fully described in his *Livros Antigos Portugueses. Early Portuguese Books, 1489-1600* (3 vols. 1929-35) Vol. II, pp. 464-73. Other editions followed in

1601, 1742, 1749, 1791 and 1843. The most convenient modern edition is that edited by Professor Marques Braga in the series Clássicos Sá da Costa (3 vols. Lisboa, 1953), which is the one used here.

4. Aubrey Fitz Gerald Bell, *Portuguese Literature* (Oxford, 1922). p. 192.
5. Henry Thomas, *Spanish and Portuguese Romances of Chivalry* (1920), pp. 138-39, 157. As Thomas points out, although Barros himself did not criticise these romances of chivalry, his contemporary and homonym, Dr. João de Barros (*c*. 1500-*c*-1580) did so. I have consulted the 1519 edition of *Claribelte* in the British Museum Library (Pressmark : C38. h8).
6. M. Menendez y Pelayo, *Origenes de la Novela*, Vol. I, p. ccxvii.
7. Francisco Rodrigues Lobo, *Corte na Aldeia e noites do inverno* (1619), a work which is most accessible in the Clássicos Sá da Costa edition by Afonso Lopes Vieira (Lisboa, 1959). Cf. pp. 10-19 for the discussion on romances of chivalry, *Clarimundo* being one of those which is specifically mentioned.
8. Jesuit letters from Goa, d. 10 Sept. 1562 and 24 Nov. 1564, in A. de Silva Rego (ed.), *Documentação para a histõria das missões do Padroado Português do Oriente, India*, IX *1562-1565* (Lisboa, 1953), pp. 60-61, 335-36.
9. I.S. Révah, *La Censure Inquisitoriale Portugaise au XVI siècle* (Lisboa, 1960), pp. 66-79; A. Baião, *A Inquisição de Goa* (2 vols., Lisboa, 1930-45), Vol. I, pp. 342-43, and Vol. II, pp. 102-03.
10. Teófilo Braga and others *apud* Marques Braga (ed.), *João de Barros. Cronica do Imperador Clarimundo*, I, XXXII-XXXIX.
11. "... E em todas estas partes, aquelas Divinas Armas e Reais Quinas serão adoradas por amor e temor" (*Clarimundo*, ed. Marques Braga, III, 102).
12. *Clarimundo* (ed. Marques Braga), III, 90-111. On p. 105 note (26) of this edition, the Island of São Lourenço (=Madagascar) is wrongly identified with Cape St. Vincent in Portugal; and on p. 108, line 22, the erroneous reading *Onde entra Simão com sua enseada* should be corrected to *ondentra Siam com sua enseada* as in the 1555 edition.
13. Other Portuguese editions in 1592, 1786, and 1852. Unlike *Clarimundo, Palmerim de Inglaterra* has a great success in foreign translations, particularly in Italy (eight editions between 1553 and 1609) and in England (four editions between 1602 and 1664). Cf. W.E. Purser, *Palmerim of England. Some remarks on this Romance and on the controversy concerning its authorship* (Dublin, 1904).

3

ROPICA PNEFMA, OR "*SPIRITUAL MERCHANDISE*", *1532*

We now have to deal with one of the most difficult works of João de Barros, and one which has been analysed and assessed very differently. An eminent Portuguese literary critic has dismissed *Ropica Pnefma* as an *obra ligeira*, "a superficial work", but he couldn't be more wrong.[1] It may have been written in the space of a few months, but then it is not a very lengthy book. In any event, far from being superficial or purely conventional, *Ropica Pnefma* is a very complex and paradoxical work, containing many passages which are obscurely worded, for reasons which we can only conjecture. Fortunately, an analytical discussion of *Ropica Pnefma* is greatly aided by the critical edition of the text provided by the late Professor I.S. Révah, and by the critical contributions of A.J. Saraiva, J.S. da Silva Dias, and other contemporary Portuguese scholars.[2]

The structure of *Ropica Pnefma* is conventional enough, being that of a typical medieval allegory, comparable in some ways with several of the *autos* of Gil Vicente, such as the *Auto da Feira* and the *Barca do Inferno*.[3] It is cast in the form a colloquy in which Understanding (*Entendimento*), Will (*Vontade*) and Time (*Tempo*) argue with Reason (*Razão*), the last-named representing human reason enlightened by the Christian revelation. Using the Erasmian device of paradox, it combines an apology for the Christian faith with a violent social satire, and with a spiritual message with strong Erasmian overtones. As mentioned above, the work was dedicated to a relative of Barros named Duarte de Resende, a Latin scholar in his own right, who had just returned to Portugal after serving as Crown Factor at the spice-island of Ternate in the Moluccas, where he had read and enjoyed

Clarimundo. Barros was then staying at his *quinta* near Pombal, in an interval between his service as Treasurer (1525-29) and Factor (1532-67) of the India and Guinea (Mina) Houses.

It is clear from the dedicatory preface, dated 25 May 1531, that Barros wrote the work between January and May of that year, ostensibly to give employment to a French printer, Germain Gaillard, who was at Coimbra with his press between January and September. For some reason, however, Gaillard did not print it until after his return to Lisbon, where it came from his press on the 8 May 1532, almost exactly a year after Barros had completed the manuscript. In this same preface, Barros states that he has composed the title from two Greek words, *Ropica* and *Pnefmaticos*, "the which, when they are grafted together, form *Ropicapnefma*, which you can call in our language *Spiritual Merchandise*".[4] Révah comments that Barros has misunderstood the passage in Plutarch from which he derived this expression—one of the many indications in his work taken as a whole that although he certainly knew a lot of Latin he probably knew only a little Greek.

In an introduction to the reader which follows his dedicatory preface to Duarte de Resende, Barros explains the aim and the outline of his work. *Will* and *Understanding* join with *Time* to undertake the role of vendors of spiritual merchandise in the form of the seven deadly sins : Pride, Avarice, Lust, Envy, Greed, Wrath and Sloth. The two former characters acquired these vices when they disobeyed *Reason* (their natural superior), and which they now want her to allow them to sell. "And with what did they buy this merchandise ? With the talents and money of the Gospel, which are the graces and the endowments that God gives to each one of us, so that we may multiply them; and when we are asked to render an account of them, we may return them increased and multiplied, like good and faithful servants. And he who is negligent, secreting the talent of his capability, or making ill use of it, will be cast into eternal fire".[5]

Barros goes on to explain that the three vendors of spiritual merchandise have to give an account of their actions during their lives to *Reason*, who is awaiting them at the castle or fortress which guards the passage to the other world at the hour of death. Those who at any time pay heed to Reason's advice and renounce their sins, doing penance for them while believing in the passion of Christ, will be received by *Reason*, and assured eventually of salvation "when the bridge of the hour of death is passed". Those who reject *Reason's* admonitions will find themselves involved in one of the three main heresies—denial of the immortality of the soul, denial of Heaven and Hell in the next world, denial that the Christian religion is the only true one.

Barros is careful to state that the greater part of the work is cast in a metaphorical and allegorical mould. The arguments advanced by *Will, Understanding* and *Time* against *Reason* "are those which any unbeliever or sinner could adduce", and should not be imputed to him.[6] Despite this disclaimer, it is obvious in some passages, and probable in others that the views advanced by *Reason's* three interlocutors—and particularly those advanced by *Time*, who has almost a moderator's role—often represent the author's real views. Contrary to the usual practice in such dialogues and colloquies, *Reason*, who is supposed to be the author's mouthpiece, does not have things all her own way. She sometimes gives evasive or unconvincing answers, or even avoids replying at all. Sometimes, indeed, she agrees with one or another of her interlocutors.[7]

The deliberately cryptical and allegorical style employed, also makes it hard to fathom the author's real meaning in some passages. So much so, that the three erudite critics who have analysed *Ropica Pnefma* most closely and convincingly come up with rather different conclusions at times. For A.J. Saraiva, *Ropica Pnefma* is "a vestige of the diffusion of the Paduan School of Averroism in Portugal, or rather of Italian materialism of the sixteenth century, and primarily intended as a rebuttal of this".[8] For I.S. Révah, *Ropica Pnefma* is "obviously" mainly directed to converting the New-Christians from their crypto-Judaic and simplified deistic religious beliefs, by persuading them of the truth of Christianity and the New Testament.[9] For J.S. da Silva Dias, the work has a much wider audience in view, following Erasmus' condemnation of scholasticism, monasticism, and external religious formalism, and echoing his pleas for a lay apostolate and for a purified inward spiritual Christianity, but reflecting also many ideals held by humanists in general.[10] Perhaps these differences of interpretation reflect the fact that Barros overdid his use of allegory and paradox; although the foregoing eminent critics are in agreement about many aspects of the work.

A brief synthesis of this singularly difficult text may not be out of place at this point. *Will* begins by presenting the spiritual and material merchandise of the seven deadly sins, with a eulogy of Pride in the first place. Pride is an indispensable inspiration for human advancement, wealth and progress, found in all courts and palaces. "And the clearest and best proof by which you can tell its greatness and goodness is that you will not find it in low and mean spirited people".[11] *Reason* rebukes *Will* for misusing her (biblical) talents and gives an allegorical version of the Ten Commandments in mercantile metaphors, adding that they can be summarised in the Gospel injunction : "Render unto Caesar the things that are Caesar's, and unto God the things that are God's" (Mark, xii). Man is composed of spirit and body, and spiritual nourishment should be given to the former, and material to the latter. *Will*, *Understanding*, and *Time* should try to multiply their talents, instead of concentrating on amassing worldly wealth, offices and dignities, as they are wrongly doing.

Will roughly rejects *Reason's* arguments as being no better than a meaningless babble "like Basque" (*Vasconços*). *Time* and *Understanding* interpose more temperately on *Will's* side. They claim that no great enterprise has been brought to a successful conclusion without the aid of pride, whether it be a world-monarchy, like the Macedonian and Roman empires, or outstanding eminence in arms and letters. *Reason* retorts by asking rhetorically what has happened to Alexander, Caesar, Plato, Aristotle, etc., all of whom were so favoured by Pride. "What reward did she give them ? Burial in Hell". All originators and inventors of false doctrines, such as Mahomet, will be punished; just as all good Christian rulers will be rewarded in this world and the next. *Understanding* digresses by asking if "the Christian prince in whose lifetime and realm artillery was invented, will be held responsible for the evil that it has done ? Should he not be excused, since presumably it was invented with the idea of using it against Muslims, the conquest of whom is praiseworthy in the eyes of God ?" *Reason* replies that good intentions can excuse many mistakes, "but in this work neither the inventor nor the patron showed good sense". The tyrant Phalaris showed better judgement when he rejected the invention of the brazen metal bull as being too cruel.[12] "See what harm has been wrought in Italy by artillery and other inhuman and immoral inventions".

Will interrupts this digression by reverting to the duality of the spirit and the flesh. She points out that this something which is accepted by all religions, whether Pagan, Jewish, Christian, and Muslim, all of which have a sacerdotal (or spiritual) and a secular (or material) estate. However, whatever the religion or the sect may be, their priests all behave as if they were motivated by material incentives rather than by spiritual values. This fact explains why physicians are more respected than priests. "Would not any sick Christian be glad to see a Jewish or a Muslim physician rather than a sad and worried confessor ?"[13] *Will* repeatedly quotes passages from Genesis to prove that concern for and study of the body is more natural than care for the soul. The Christian clergy live by the altar and do very well out of it.

Reason naturally rebutts these scandalous allegations, and as Révah points out, launches into what is, in effect, a summary of the cosmology of Raymond Sebond's *Liber Creaturarum* (1436).[14] She sketches the panorama of nature in four classes or categories, ranging from inanimate objects such as stones and metals, through the vegetable and the animal kingdoms to the fourth and noblest, which is Man, the only sentient being endowed with a free will. Man is a microcosm of Nature, as the Ancients well understood. Mankind likewise has a hierarchical subdivision, with the "artisans, peasants, and traders (*tratantes*)" at the bottom of the social scale. However, although these form the lowest class in a commonwealth, they are the most necessary for its maintenance "since they are the columns which sustain the whole edifice. For thanks to their sweat, the priest prays, the knight defends, and the lord rules".[15]

Reason reproaches *Will* and *Understanding* for having abandoned the stronghold of the eternal God and joined His enemies, becoming "so rude and ignorant" that they forget their own higher nature. After further reproaches to her interlocutors, *Reason* sketches the spiritual history of mankind from the first sacrifice of Abel to the birth of "the Light of the world". Christ, in saying : "Blessed are the poor in spirit; for theirs is the kingdom of Heaven" (Matthew, 5, iii) did not tolerate Pride but denounced it. He gave the eight beatitudes which he promised in the Sermon on the Mount,[16] which are just the opposite of what *Will, Time* and *Understanding* are trying to sell.

After some discussion on the immortality or otherwise of the soul, the topic switches to a consideration of the sum of human knowledge. *Understanding* boasts that : "in the basic elements of the whole of science, which are the three tongues of Greek, Latin and Hebrew, I learnt all the precepts and rhetorical figures and colours which enable me to declaim, to orate, and to compose in prose and in verse". He also claims to be expert in the occult sciences, in medicine, in jurisprudence, in philosophy and in theology. The successive exposition of each of these in turn, gives João de Barros the opportunity of satirising through the mouths of his characters, astrologists, physicians, lawyers, scholastic theologians, and worldly preachers. He boasts of the Portuguese discoveries by making *Understanding* say : "As regards cosmography, with the vastness of the worlds discovered by the enlightened (*esclarecidos*) kings of Portugal, if Ptolemey, Strabo, Pomponius, Pliny, or Solinus could come here now with their three paltry leaves (maps) they would all be reduced to confusion and shame; for I would show them that the regions of the world which they did not know about were vaster than the three into which they divided those that they did".[17]

Understanding also boasts about the knowledge he has acquired from frequenting the Court, which gives João de Barros a pretext for satirizing certain social classes, including a particularly violent denunciation of the worldly higher clergy, "who, like accursed shepherds, roam around the fields, battening on the sweat of others without praying for anyone, buying female slaves, giving misleading advice to those seeking good counsel, raising greyhounds and not orphans, and, instead of perusing holy scriptures, they have racks of hunting-pikes, stacks of playing-cards, dice to throw, rescripts to inherit, denying their ecclesiastical dress and office, whereby they will provoke the wrath of the Lord to despoil them of their natural possessions".[18]

The discussion of the immortality of the soul is then resumed, giving *Will* the opportunity of denying that the soul "is an intellectual and immortal substance", but rather something that acts more like the weight of a clock, which only functions for as long as the mechanism is wound up (*i.e.*, for as long as the body functions). This and other Averroistic-influenced ideas are rejected by *Reason,* who argues *inter alia* : "God did not make such a great work as this world, nor the souls which are even greater, merely to have such a brief existence as is the life". She quotes pagan philosophers as well as Christian, in order to prove the immortality of the soul. This part of the discussion concludes with *Time* admitting that the soul is immortal, but doubting whether there are a Heaven and a Hell where rewards and punishments are meted out after death.

The discussion then turns on this problem, with *Reason* arguing that the adherents of all religions believe in rewards and punishments in the after-world or next life. But her interlocutors are not entirely convinced, and *Will* flatly declines to be impressed by childish and fabulous fears of Hell. She wonders whether pagans, or Jews, or Christians, or Muslims have the true idea about belief in God. In reality, all branches of mankind prefer material merchandise to the spiritual variety ; and they all fervently cultivate the seven deadly sins, which *Will* proceeds to extoll. Covetousness and money are the mainsprings of power. Priests of the different religions have invented such fables as the Elysian fields, the Land of Promise, rivers flowing with milk and honey, the Christian Paradise, etc , etc., together with various forms of Hell and Purgatory, in order to keep the lower classes quiet and submissive.[19] Jealous of the extraordinary success of the ecclesiastical establishment, the secular authorities have likewise developed their own systems of laws and taxation for the same ends, thus reducing the common people to slavery on the pretext of preserving the security of the state.

Time, *Will*, and *Understanding* then engage in a rather

abstruse discussion about the fundamentals of law, the principles of government, and the literary quarrel between the Ancients and the Moderns, with occasional interventions by *Reason* on the side of *Time*. This discussion gives Barros an opportunity of satirising lawyers and physicians. Laws and medicine are both the better for being sparingly used. The fewer medicines people take, the better health they enjoy : "less laws, fewer lawyers and fewer lawsuits ; fewer lawsuits, greater peace. Few physicians bleed themselves in their own illnesses, but they are very prodigal of blood-letting when treating others" (*Poucos medicos se sangram nas suas infirmidades, e nas vidas alheias são mui soltos em obras*).[20]

Reason has great difficulty in convincing *Will* of the superiority of Christianity over all other religions in general, and over Judaism in particular. At one point, she exclaims in exasperation : "Before we go any further in this discussion, you must choose one of two things : accept the Old Testament altogether, or else reject it entirely. You want to use the Holy Scripture like a palm-tree, which gives you sweet, bitter, or whatever else you want. Why don't you believe in the creation of the world and the saving of mankind after the Flood, as described by Ovid ?

Will : Because it seems fabulous to me, and that of Moses more truthful.

Reason : Do you believe everything that Moses wrote ?

Will : As regards the creation of the world, yes. But don't try to persuade me with allegories, but only with the literal sense and natural reason, if you have it.

Reason : So be it !"[21]

She then launches into a lengthy exposition of orthodox Christian doctrine. God is not unjust. In all the stages of history, Man has been able to save himself successively through the law of Nature, the scriptural law of the Old Testament, and the Christian law of Grace. Arguments derived from "natural reason" and from the "reason of the Faith" are deployed, and reinforced with numerous citations from pre-Christian classical authors who proclaimed the existence of Heaven and Hell, including Ovid, Catullus, Seneca, Horace, and Plato. At the end of *Reason's* harangue, *Will* states that she is now convinced of the existence of

Heaven and Hell, and of rewards and punishments in the next world; but she challenges *Reason* to prove that Christianity is superior to all other religions in general and to Judaism in particular.[22]

We now reach a crucial stage in the Colloquy. *Will* opens the argument by giving a comparative exposition of the four great religions of Mankind, Paganism, Judaism, Christianity and Islam, from which she deduces implicitly the inferiority of Christianity and the superiority of Judaism. *Reason* of course, refutes *Will's* arguments one by one; pointing out, *inter alia*, that after Christ's death and resurrection Christianity was spread over the greater part of the globe "by twelve rustic and cowardly men", who had denied and forsaken Him in His lifetime.[23] This astounding result was achieved, not by force of arms, "like the people of Moses did, and the sect of Mohamed, nor by the favour of princes, as did many heretics past and present, but only through the fervour of the faith and of the Holy Spirit which spoke through them". On the other hand, the Hebrews, so extolled by *Will* for their denial of Christ, were reduced to the lowest stages of degradation and humiliation. After the destruction of Jerusalem, "they were and still are scattered throughout the world, enslaved, subjugated, and despised by all the nations thereof".

At one point, *Understanding* intervenes to argue that Christ violated the Jewish Sabbath and other religious and legal observances, so he was obviously a false Messiah and not the true one. *Reason* refutes this contention with quotations from the Old and New Testaments, incidentally putting in a plug for Portugal's expansion of the faith to the uttermost ends of the earth and from sea to shining sea.[24] *Understanding* is still far from being convinced, reproaching *Reason* for denigrating the Old Testament and for accepting the "fables" of the New.

This remonstrance gives *Reason* a pretext for launching into a vitriolic denunciation of the Old Testament as the work of bloody-minded and bloody-handed Jews. "Can one call Holy Scripture that which is full of idolatries, adulteries, robberies, murders, and as many other evils and lewdnesses as there are in the world?"[25] Even many profane histories would blush to contain some of the scabrous details in the

Old Testament. What about the Jewish Temple of God, which was converted into a butcher's shambles, with all the bloody animal sacrifices which were continually offered there—something which in civilized cities was done outside the walls? Was God so bloodthirsty that He rejoiced in these bloody sacrifices and wanted Himself and His priests to be like butcher-boys, "which is the basest and lewdest calling that there is?"

In Christ's Law, on the other hand, there was no bloodshed save His own, which He gave for the salvation of mankind. What a difference between the life and works of Christ and of Moses! "He pardoned all offenders against Him at His death, saying: 'Father, forgive them, for they know not what they do'" (Luke, xxiii). Moses was so vindictive that he killed an innocent Egyptian, who was guilty of nothing more than arguing with a common or garden Jew (*um Hebreu do povo*). He allowed the Jews to practice usury, to repudiate their wives, to marry near relatives, "and to keep three hundred concubines, with other liberalities in conformity with their national character". Christ, on the other hand, denounced usury, divorce, adultery, and the maxim of exacting an eye for an eye and a tooth for a tooth, urging His followers to turn the other cheek to aggressors.[26]

This astonishing denunciation of the Old Testament as the equivalent of what nowadays would be called a "blue" book, provokes *Time* to say that *Reason* sounds more like Erasmian Folly than Portuguese Reason (*Mais me parece, pois tão desarrazoada estás que te convêm o nome de Sandice Erasma que Razão Portugueza*). He also points out that Christ, in order to authorise His own Law, had validated the Old. Did He not say to the Jews: "For had ye believed Moses, ye would have believed me; for he wrote of me" (John, v, 46). *Reason* gives a long and (to my mind) rather unconvincing answer to *Time's* last question, implying that the Old Testament must not be taken literally but in an allegorical sense as a prefiguration of the New.[27] After much further discussion, *Will* eventually states that she and her companions acknowledge the divinity of Christ as the true Messiah. She adds that in reality they were bound to do so both by faith and the baptism which they had received. She only wanted to test

Reason's knowledge, and now asks the latter not to detain them any longer with a lengthy examination of their merchandise.

Reason makes the rejoinder that if they wish to multiply their talents, they must burn their accursed merchandise in the fires of penitence; for to believe in Christ without implementing His precepts is going along the road to Hell. At this point, *Understanding* intervenes with the observation that no single human being ever can or has imitated Christ perfectly. *Reason* then defines the imitation of Christ by recalling the words of Jesus : "Learn of me, for I am meek and lowly in heart" (Matthew, xi, 29). He did not say "be like me" but "learn from me". If a Negro is named John White (João Branco), that does not make him white in colour; but if he becomes white through some natural process, then the name would fit him absolutely.[28] Thus, if sinners sincerely repent and through tears of penitence become whiter than snow, they will be pardoned and become inheritors of Jesus Christ—like the few who have never bowed the knee to Baal, and like the many who have renounced the sinful merchandise to which *Time*, *Understanding* and *Will* still cling. There is some further discussion on various themes, including Age and Youth, Christian pacifism, and education, with *Time* making another vitriolic attack on laws and lawyers.[29]

Reason finally loses her patience and launches into a long harangue, emphasising that, in order to love God, one must hate and despise the world. She again reminds her interlocutors with a wealth of citations that it is not only the sages and prophets of Israel, the apostles and the evangelists of Christianity, Christ Himself, and the Fathers of the Church, who have urged mankind to seek salvation through repentance of sins. The same appeal was made by pagan philosophers, including Seneca, Ovid and Plautus, none of whom were illuminated by the Scriptures and by divine grace. For those who do repent, salvation is certain, as *Reason* proves with many more citations from both Testaments, including Matthew, XI, 28-30 : "Come unto me, all ye that labour and are heavy laden, and I wlll give you rest. Take my yoke upon you, and learn of me; for I am meek and lowly in heart, and ye shall find rest unto your souls. For my yoke is easy and my burden is light".

Despite *Reason's* impassioned eloquence, it seems that her interlocutors still find it difficult to accept her conclusions entirely. The colloquy concludes with a speech by *Time*, who admits that *Reason's* arguments are "holy, just and honest"; but he and his erring companions can hardly renounce their beloved merchandise without more ado. "The day is far spent and the night is at hand". Since the night hours afford a suitable time for contemplation, *Time* tells *Reason* that he will use this interval to try to persuade his two hesitant companions to meditate more deeply over the truth of what she had said, for it is always difficult to make a sudden change in the habits of a lifetime.[30]

In his penetrating analysis of this complex and paradoxical work, I.S. Révah pointed out that it can hardly be by chance that the only two sixteenth-century works explicitly cited in *Ropica Pnefma* are the *Colloquies* (1521) and *In Praise of Folly* of Erasmus. Révah is undoubtedly right in stating that João de Barros, far from being always a feeble Erasmian as Carolina Michaëlis de Vasconcellos and others have alleged, ("João de Barros, que sempre foi fraco erasmista mesmo no Tratado de *Mercadoria Espiritual*") was strongly influenced by the Dutch humanist and reproduced many of his ideas. This is a contention with which both A.J. Saraiva and J.S. da Silva Dias agree.[31] It is not merely that Barros has utilised the essentially Erasmian technique combining paradox and colloquy, but his forms of anti-Judaism, anti-scholasticism, social criticism, and his advocacy of Christian pacifism, all bear strong resemblances to those of Erasmus. Like Erasmus, João de Barros evidently had a marked dislike for most of the books of the Old Testament. He vigorously attacked formalism and scholasticism on the one hand, while extolling the pure and evangelical content of the New Testament. The message of Christ and of the Apostles is simplicity and peace. The supreme science is the imitation of Christ, and all the rest is vanity.

Although Barros, as a patriotic Portuguese and as the potential author of the *Decades*, may imply in *Ropica Pnefma* that Portuguese expansion by force of arms in Africa and the East is justified, this crusading zeal receives no explicit support in this work, as it did in *Clorimundo*. The emphasis in *Ropica Pnefma* is rather on peaceful missionary evangelism and on the utility of the voyages of discovery. One may agree with A.J. Saraiva when he claims that *Ropica Pnefma* is, among other things, "the completest and most explicit manifestation of Portuguese Erasmianism".[32] As Révah has pointed out, while primarily indebted to Erasmus, Barros also owned a good deal to the previously mentioned *Liber Creaturarum* (1436) of Raymond Sébond, and, in all probability, to the *De incertitude et vanitate* (Antwerp, 1530) of Henri Cornelis Agrippa (1486-1535). This last-named work has several themes in common with those of *Ropica Pnefma*, and there is an affinity of spirit between the two which would derive from their Erasmian origin.[33]

It may be added that many of the digressions in *Ropica Pnefma* have a charm and interest of their own, which add to the originality of the work, and bring to the reader's mind some parallel in later literature. For instance, at one point *Reason* exclaims : "Some people *have* already adopted as their motto Might is Right. One may ask when two sides fight with each other, who is the judge of their cause ? The side which mobilises the most soldiers and uses the most gunpowder". This anticipates many similar *obiter dicta*, such as Padre António Vieira, S.J.'s, 'God is on the side of the most musketeers"; Napoleon's, "God is on the side of the big battalions"; and Stalin's "How many divisions has the Pope ?"[34]

Ropica Pnefma, it may be recalled, was written at what might be termed the crest of the wave of the Portuguese Renaissance and Humanism. It was composed in the same year that Gil Vicente's most anti-clerical play, *Jubileu de Amores* (Love's Jubilee) was performed in the house of the Portuguese envoy at Brussels. Five years later, the Holy Office of the Inquisition was introduced into Portugal. Although *Ropica Pnefma* was not banned by the Inquisition until 1581, no other anti-clerical work of this kind was published in the interval, if we except Gil Vicente's *Auto da Feira*, which was included in the *Compilaçam* of 1562.

Certainly no such work could have been published in Portugal after the mid-sixteenth century.

Although *Ropica Pnefma* seems to have had curiously little impact, judging by the very few references to it in Portuguese literature of the next 350 years,[35] nevertheless it must rank as one of the most singular and important works published in Portugal during the old régime. In fact, I would venture to claim that it can vie in this respect with another and much better known (though very different) work, the *Peregrination* of Fernão Mendes Pinto.[36]

NOTES

1. It is kinder to withhold his name; but it is not unfair to say that Portuguese (and all other) critics did not appreciate the real importance of *Ropica Pnefma*, until Professor I.S. Révah's work drew attention to it in the 1950s.
2. I.S. Révah, *João de Barros. Ropica Pnefma*, (2 vols., facsimile reproduction and modernised text, Lisboa, 1952-55), *Ibidem*, "Le Colloque *Ropicapnefma* de João de Barros. Gènese, structure et technique", in "*Mélanges offerts à Marcel Bataillon par les Hispanistes Français*" (Bordeaux, 1962), pp. 572-92; *Ibidem*, "Antiquité et Christianisme, Anciens et Modernes dans l'oeuvre de João de Barros", in *Revue Philosophique de la France et de l'Etranger*, Vol. 00, pp. 165-85 (Paris, 1966). Unfortunately, Professor Révah died before completing his projected work on the *Ropica Pnefma*, but all his published articles on João de Barros and related subjects are due to be reprinted in a single volume edited by Professor Eugenio Asensio, as the latter informed me (November, 1973). See also António José Saraiva, *História da Cultura em Portugal*, Vol. II (Lisboa, 1955), pp. 563-606, "Averroismo e Erasmismo da *Rópica Pnefma*"; J.S. da Silva Dias, *A Política Cultural da época de Dom João III*, Vol. I (Coimbra 1969), pp. 257-86.
3. For the Vicentine *autos* of the *Fair* and the *Ship of Hell* see J.H. Parker, *Gil Vicente* (1967), pp. 54-66, 94-95, and the editions there cited.
4. ". . . ofereço-vos este pomo que naceo destes dous ramos gregos : a um chamam *Ropica* e a outro *Pnefmaticos*. Os quais enxertados um em outro, lançaram de si *Ropicapnefma*, a que em nossa linguagem podeis chamar *Mercadoria Espiritual*" (p. 6 of I.S. Révah's 1955 edition). Although Barros wrote his hybrid invention as one word, and it is so printed in the edition of 1532, I have followed Révah's edition of 1955 in printing it as two.
5. The parable of the talents is in Matthew, XXV, 14-30, in the King James Anglican Authorised Version, which I have used in these

notes for facilitating references; but Barros, of course, was using a pre-1532 Roman Catholic Latin Bible.

6. "Que a maior parte desta obra vai em metáfora, e que as cousas e autoridades que a Vontade, Intendimento e Tempo arguem contra a Razão são as que qualquer infiel e pecador pode arguir, e, com esta condição, sem lhe dar outro crédito, as receba. Esta e a principal cousa que encomendo e peço àqueles que tanto não alcançam" (ed. Révah, 1955, p. 7)
7. For instance, after *Understanding* has delivered a vitriolic attack on abuses prevalent among courtiers and the higher clergy (pp. 51-56), *Reason* says that this is sorrowful news to her, since she has been absent for so long from such courtly circles; but she adds that the criticisms may well be justified, "since the flesh is so corrupt that it infects the pillars of the Law" (*op cit.*, p. 56).
8. A.J. Saraiva, *História da Cultura em Portugal*, Vol. II (1955), pp. 576-79, "O Averroismo paduano na *Ropica Pnefma*".
9. I.S. Révah, "João de Barros" (*Revista do Livro*, Rio de Janeiro, No. 9, March 1958, pp. 61-71, and especially pp. 64-65). Cf. also Révah's studies cited in note (2) above. For a somewhat different standpoint see Theda van Royen, "Contributo para a Revisão do Conceito Erasmismo e a sua Influência na Literatura Portuguesa do século XVI com base na *Rópica Pnefma* de João de Barros", in *Ocidente. Revista Portuguesa Mensal*, No. 354, Vol. LXXXIII (Lisboa, October 1967), pp. 1-33, and especially pp. 24-33 of the *Suplemento*.
10. J.S. da Silva Dias, *A Política Cultural da época de D. João III*, Vol. I (Coimbra, 1969), pp. 257-80, and especially pp. 273-74. A similar viewpoint is taken by another exceptionally well-qualified authority, José V. de Pina Martins, *Sobre o conceito do Humanismo e alguns aspectos histórico-doutrinários da Cultura Portuguesa* (reprint edition from the *Arquivos do Centro Cultural Português*, Vol. II, Paris, 1970), especially p. 86.
11. "E o mais claro e certo sinal per que conhecerás sua bondade é não se achar em baixos e temorosos espiritos" ed. Révah, p. 20).
12. Barros has slipped up here, as contrary to what *Reason* alleges, Phalaris *did* make use of the hollow brazen bull to roast criminals alive, beginning with the inventor of this infernal machine.
13. "Qual foi o médico judeu ou mouro que não fosse a sua vista mais saudável a um cristão infermo que a dum triste e carregado confessor ?" (ed. Révah, p. 28).
14. Raymond Sebond, or Sibinde, apparently of Catalan origin, professor and (in due course) Rector of the University of Toulouse. His *Liber creaturarum* was begun in 1434 and finished 11 Feb. 1436, the author dying at Toulouse on the 29 April of that year. See I.S. Révah, "Le Colloque *Ropicanefma*", p. 576 *n* (13), and the sources there quoted.

15. ". . . mecânicos, lavradores e tratantes. Os quais, dado que sejam a mais baixa calidade em as repúbricas, peró necessária pera a sua conservação por serem ñas colunas que sustêm todo o edéficio. Ca, mediante o suor de todos estes, o sacerdote reza, o cavaleiro defende, o senhor governa" (ed. Révah, p. 33).
16. The blessings pronounced by Our Lord at the beginning of the Sermon on the Mount, of which there are nine in the Anglican Authorized Version (Matthew, V, 3-16).
17. Ed. Révah, p. 42.
18. ". . . com que indinarão ao Senhor pera os despojar de suas materiais possissoes" (ed. Révah, p. 55). Perhaps this is an allusion to the suppression of the monasteries and the seizure of their goods by Henry VIII in England, a precedent followed by Protestant rulers in other countries.
19. "As outras vaidades de Campos Eliseos, Terra de Promissão, rios de mel e manteiga, e Paraiso como os Cristãos entendem, com as penas a estes contrarias, são espantos e temores d'abusão que os sacerdotes destas opinioes inventaram pera enfrear o povo rústico e o trazerem à obediencia de seus preceitos" (ed. Révah, p. 72).
20. "Poucos médicos se sangram nas suas infirmidades, e nas vidas alheas são mui soltos em obras" (ed. Révah, p. 79).
21. Ed. Révah, p. 85.
22. Ed. Révah, pp. 85-90.
23. "E nós vemos que ela (Christ's death) descobrio mais sua divinidade, pois por meio de doze homans rústicos e covardes, e de tão pouca fé em vida deste mesmo Christo, foi depois a maior parte do mundo debaixo Seu jugo" (ed. Révah, pp. 100-101).
24. "Nesta espécia e redondeza é Cristo, verdadeiro Deos e Messias, adorado dos Etiopes e reis de Társis em os sumptuosos templos que os cristianíssimos Reis de Portugal fizeram. Aos quais, com justa causa, podes chamar novos apóstolos, pois levaram o nome de Cristo a ser adorado, celebrado e louvado de mar a mar, té os termos da redondeza das terras, em que se cumpre a monarquia que lhe David dá espiritual e successivamente nesta primeira vinda" (*Psalm* 72). Ed. Révah, pp. 106-07.
25. "Santa Escritura se pode chamar a que está chea de idolatrias, adultérios, roubos, homícidios e de quantos males e torpezas há no mundo ?" (ed. Révah, pp. 109-110 for this and what follows).
26. "E Moses veo na maior opressão que eles tiveram, e consentio-lhe onzenar, repudiar mulheres, casar com parentas, e trezentas mancebas, com outras larguezas conformes à sua condição. E Cristo reprendia a onzena, o repùdio, o adùltério, dente por dente, olho por olho, e mandou aparar ũa face a quem desse na outra" (ed. Révah, pp. 110-111).
27. Ed. Révah pp. 111-15. Cf. also A.J. Saraiva's comments in ***História da Cultura em Portugal,*** Vol. II, pp. 573 74, 579.

28. "Não te pareça que por a um Negro chamarem João Branco, logo lhe fica o cor do apelido; quando tiver este acidente branco, convir-lhe-á naturalmente" (ed. Révah, p. 122).
29. Ed. Révah, pp. 127-28. For an analysis of the denigrating references to lawyers and the legal profession in *Ropica Pnefma* and in other sixteenth-century Portuguese humanistic works, see Nuno J. Espinosa Gomes da Silva, *Humanismo e Direito em Portugal no século XVI* (Lisboa, 1964), pp. 95-109.
30. "O dia é passado, a noite vem-se, e porque nela os espíritos se recolhem mais em si pera julgar as dúvidas que contra nossa multiplicação moves, fica-te em boa hora, que a Vontade e Intendimento querem haver novo conselho sobre os teus" (ed. Révah, p. 151).
31. I.S. Révah, "Le Colloque Ropicapnefma de João de Barros" (1962), pp. 588-92; A.J. Saraiva *História da Cultura em Portugal*, II, 570-76, 601-06; J.S. da Silva Dias, *A Politica Cultural da época de Dom João III*, Vol. I, pp. 272-80; Theda van Royen, "Contributo para a Revisão do Conceito Erasmismo. . . com base na *Rópica Pnefma*", pp. 28-33.
32. Ed. Révah, pp. 106-07; A.J. Saraiva, *História da Cultura em Portugal* II, 564, 592-93.
33. I.S. Révah, "Le Colloque *Ropicapnefma* de João de Barros" (1962), p. 590.
34. "Já alguns trouxeram por letra de sua divisa : 'O direito nas armas'. Pergunta ora quando uns contendem com os outros : quem é o juiz de sua causa ? O poder que mais soldados ajunta e mais pólvora despende" (ed. Révah, p. 141). For António Vieira S.J.'s similar observation : "É prática mui ordinária entre os políticos que sempre Deus se poe da parte dos mais mosqueteiros", see his "Sermão pelo bom sucessos das nossas armas" preached in 1645, *apud* Hermâni Cidade (ed.), *Pe António Vieira. Obras Escolhidas*, Vol. X, *Sermões* (I), p. 235 (Lisboa, 1954).
35. Manuel Severim de Faria refers to it (*Discursos*, 1624, fls. 27-8) in terms which indicate that he had read it, although it was a prohibited book. As a highly respected and influential ecclesiastic, he could have got permission from the Inquisitors to do so, and he may even have had it in his own library. He explains that it was banned, not because it contained any harmful doctrine, but because ill-intentioned persons might misuse it.
36. For some of the controversial aspects of the *Peregrinaçam*, see A.J. Saraiva, *História da Cultura em Portugal*, Vol. III (1962), pp. 343, 491-96, and Domingos Mauricio S.J.'s critical review of Saraiva's 1961 edition of the *Peregrinaçam* in *Brotéria*, Vol. LXXIV (June, 1962), pp. 637-50. I have recently (1968) seen an unpublished University of California, Los Angeles, Ph.D. thesis of 1972 by Debora Catz, "Iconoclasm as literary technique : a study of the satiric devices used in the *Peregrinação de Fernão Mendes Piuto*".

I understand this will shortly appear at Lisbon in a Portuguese translation. There is no good annoted text of the *Peregrinaçam* by an Orientalist in any language that I know of; but the interested reader may be referred to Maurice Collis, *The Grand Peregrination. Being the life and adventures of Fernão Mendes Pinto* (London, 1949), pending the publication of the work by Debora Catz, which I feel sure will supersede it.

4

PANEGYRICAL AND POLEMICAL WORKS, 1533-44

The three works discussed in this chapter, two panegyrics of royal personages and an anti-Jewish treatise, were all written at a period between the publication of *Ropica Pnefma* and that of the group of grammatical and didactic works in 1539-40. None of these three were published in the lifetime of of João de Barros; and for that reason likewise they may be considered together as posthumous works.

(a) *Panegyric of King John III, 1533*

The panegyric, as its name implies, did not purport to be a piece of objective history, "warts and all", but rather a eulogy, often unrestrained or even grotesquely flattering, of the exalted personage to whom it was addressed. Derived from classical models, it was a very popular genre among the humanists of the Renaissance. It gave scope for them to display their knowledge of the classics, to declaim in well-rounded and eloquent phrases, and to flatter actual or potential patrons with that gratitude which is defined as a lively sense of favours to come. There was also the moral justification, which João de Barros cites as the opening sentence of this panegyric, that these eulogies would inspire some of the audience to do other praiseworthy deeds, so as to become the subjects of panegyrics in their turn.[1] They also, of course, served the function of a "public-relations" exercise on behalf of the persons to whom they were addressed.

At the beginning of the 1533 panegyric, Barros even advanced the claim, which he probably did not intend his audience to take too seriously, that a panegyric was morally superior to a chronicle or a history. "For whereas the panegyric faithfully reproduces what it sees and represents it to the eyes, history, for the most part, is only hearsay and consigned to the memory".[2] In the same passage, he states that the panegyric derives ultimately from the heroic poetry and the ballads sung to commemorate the noble deeds of great men in Antiquity and in the Middle Ages. He praises the Turks for continuing this custom; adding that if it were followed in Western Europe, "we would derive more advantage from such music than from sentimental songs and love lyrics, if I am not mistaken".[3]

From the context of this particular panegyric, it is clear that it was delivered before King John III and his court at Evora, some time in the year 1533. Barros had already entered on his responsible duties as Factor of the India and Guinea Houses at Lisbon; but presumably he would have made a trip to Evora for this special occasion, just as Gil Vicente, "goldsmith and master of the balance", did for the purpose of staging some of his plays. Although the king was then actively engaged in negotiating with Rome for the establishment of a Portuguese branch of the Inquisition, he was also still hoping to attract Erasmus to Portugal.[4] The publication of the singularly outspoken *Ropica Pnefma* in the previous year obviously had done Barros no harm in the eyes of the pious monarch (*o piedoso*), despite its strongly anti-clerical passages and despite the bitterness of much of its satire of those in high places.

Unlike the deliberately paradoxical and often enigmatic style affected in the *Ropica Pnefma*, this panegyric is written in a flowing and straightforward prose, although it is full of sententious observations and moral reflections. But while no opportunity is lost of extolling John III for his real or presumed virtues, Barros has certainly used the occasion to inculcate some ideas of his own, as well as some of those of Erasmus. Révah has pointed out—what Rodrigues Lapa seems to have missed—that Barros had certainly reflected on and utilized Erasmus' *Institutio Principis Christiani* (*Institutions of a Christian Prince*, 1516), even if he did not specifically quote it. Barros does have several references to Plutarch's *Lives*, as well as to Pliny's panegyric of the Emperor Trajan which was confessedly one of his models.[5] There is a wealth of allusions to other classical authors, which enable Barros to display his knowledge of Greek and Roman mythology, history, and literature. In contrast to *Ropica Pnefma*, there are no allusions to the New Testament, but several to the Old.

One of the Erasmian echoes is the warm advocacy of peace. King John III is praised for making peace the cornerstone of his European foreign policy. "What panegyric, what praise does not Your Highness deserve, since you have implemented so perfectly ever since the commencement of your reign anything connected with such an outstanding virtue ?"[6] While the greater number of Christian princes are constantly warring with each other, the King of Portugal has been most careful to maintain peace at home and in Europe, and he has been blessed by God, accordingly. Warming to this theme, Barros proclaims : There is no wordly triumph nor victory which can be compared with the benefits derived from a true peace. Therefore, those Christian princes who fight and wage war with one another, go against the peace which Our Lord so much commended to His disciples, and in His name to the whole Catholic Church. When they give vent to their passions at the cost of the blood of their vassals, they rend in pieces the robe of Christ, in which there is no seam nor join. Let Your Highness, on the other hand, continue as you are doing with your very holy intentions of waging war on the unbelievers and Muslims of Africa, and, moved by most holy zeal, convert Ethiopia and Arabia, Persia and India, to the true faith of Christ".[7]

Unlike *Ropica Pnefma*, where, as we have seen, the overseas expansion of militant Christianity is severely muted, here and elsewhere in this panegyric, Barros reverts to the crusading line taken in *Clarimundo*. After another impassioned plea for peace at home and in Europe, he adds : "I do not mean to criticise here the concept of war against unbelievers and the enemies of our holy faith; for this, being a just war, is advantageous and brings great prestige to a Christian king". But any other kind of war, unless it be a purely defensive one against unprovoked aggression, should be avoided like the plague.[8]

When he urged King John III to keep the peace at any price in Europe, João de Barros was preaching to the already converted. As the panegyrist himself observed later, the

Piedoso had gone to great lengths in order to avoid war with France, despite the enormous damage done to Portuguese shipping in the Atlantic by French privateers, both Calvinist and Catholic. In fact, if there ever was an attitude of turning the other cheek, it was exemplified in John III's attitude to the French monarchy. Such measures as he took, largely ineffectual, were purely defensive at sea and purely diplomatic on land. But Barros heartily approved of this policy of appeasement, arguing that it derived from the desire to spare the king's subjects the horrors of war, and was evidence of strength rather than of weakness.[9]

We probably have here not only a reflection of the *Institution of a Christian Prince*, but also of the similar sentiments expressed in Erasmus' earlier addresses, such as that delivered to Prince Philip the Fair in Brussels at the request of the States of Brabant in 1504, and in his *Enchiridion militis christiani* (1505). In all those works, Erasmus urged ruling princes to follow a peaceful and paternalistic policy, which would favour the welfare of their subjects and spare them the horrors of warfare.[10]

King John is also praised for his abstemiousness in not drinking wine, an admirable trait which he shared with his brothers and inherited from his father, Manuel the Fortunate, as Barros rightly notes. Solomon, Plato, Plutarch, Octavian, Cyrus, are all quoted as inculcating temperance in a ruler. Here again, Barros was preaching to the already converted. With the solitary exception of the half-mad and spastic king Dom Afonso VI (reigned 1656-1667), the Portuguese monarchs all vastly preferred water to wine; and, for that matter, the Portuguese people have always had the reputation of being the soberest in Europe.[11]

King John is also extolled and no doubt correctly, for his moderation in food and in dress; and for his addiction to the chase—the sport of kings, as Barros notes. However, he is careful to add : "but although this is a laudable exercise, and Your Highness practises it in moderation and in due seasons, yet you deserve incomparably greater praise for your continual and toilsome exercise of good government, and in maintaining great peace and justice in your kingdom;

whereby you alone have a hard life and all the rest of us live quietly at our ease".[12]

Adverting to King John III's generous patronage of letters and of scholarship, Barros rightly emphasised how much the progress of learning in Portugal was due to the royal initiative. He alluded to the king's intention to reform and reorganize the University, which would still further foster the development of arts and sciences.[13] He emphasised that there was no dichotomy between arts and letters; and that, on the contrary, both were equally essential for the well-being of the nation, and that many famous captains and warriors had likewise been renowned as men of letters. Alluding to the *bolseiros del Rei*, Barros declaimed : "What shall I say of the youths whom Your Highness at your own cost and charges sent and sends daily to the University of Paris, in order to study the liberal arts and sacred theology, so that the prestige of your kingdom may be increased no less in letters than in other virtues ? The Emperor Trajan is praised for having ordered 5,000 poor Roman boys to be brought up at his expense. But Your Highness is much worthier of greater praise than Trajan, for as much as progress in letters and learning is much more to be esteemed than any other upbringing".[14]

Among the moral reflections with which Barros freely interlards this panegyric, is a warning against the use of foreign mercenaries. He points out that such hired troops are apt to turn on their employers, of which he gives many historical examples, including the sack of Rome in 1527. "Wherefore, the prince who wishes his people to be strong, will make war using his compatriots, remembering that no commander made great conquests save with his own countrymen. And if the Emperor Charles V gained such victories in our times over the King of France, and took him prisoner in a battle won by his captains, the principal reason for this was that he used chiefly native Spaniards, his compatriots; while the King of France, on the contrary, relied largely on Swiss and Italians".[15]

In the course of this lengthy panegyric, João de Barros may sometimes have exaggerated the virtues of King John III, and, naturally enough, he said nothing about his failings. But it would be a mistake to dismiss this panegyric as a piece of empty flattery, or as merely inspired by gratitude to a monarch who had generously patronised the panegyrist. King John III was a paternal ruler with a genuine concern for the welfare of his subjects. A sixteenth-century Englishman who was under no such personal obligations to the *Piedoso*, wrote some twenty-five years later : "This John King of Portugal was of nature very gentle and courteous, and won all men's minds unto him through his integrity and godliness. He enlarged the bournes of his kingdom even to the uttermost ends of the earth".[16]

(b) *Panegyric of the Princess Dona Maria, 1545*

This panegyric is less than half the length of that delivered in honour of King John III, which must have been a relief to most of the audience—assuming that both speeches were delivered in full and not expanded after the event. The Infanta Dona Maria had received the seigniory of Viseu and Torres Vedras from her royal half-brother in January 1545. This address was presumably delivered by João de Barros in his capacity as an illustrious native son of the former town, shortly after that date.[17]

The text naturally follows a similar pattern to that of the preceding one. The Infanta's virtues and accomplishments, including her knowledge of Latin and her skill in music, are lauded to the skies; and no mention is made of her human failings (if any). As indicated in chapter 1, Dona Maria was in fact an exceptionally well-educated and talented princess, so that Barros' encomium of her scholarship is certainly not much exaggerated.[18] As with the panegyric addressed to the king, there is a wealth of classical erudition displayed in this text, balanced by frequent references to the Old Testament, but none to the New. The influence of Erasmus is not so evident as in the earlier panegyric, but it is certainly there. Barros makes explicit acknowledgement to *In Praise of Folly* (*Encomium Moriae*), one of the great humanist's works which was under severe criticism from the increasingly powerful orthodox and reactionary circles at that time.[19]

In this panegyric, the advantages of peace are not stressed to the same extent as in the former one. There is a long paean of praise to Portuguese expansion overseas and to the temporal and spiritual conquests achieved during the reign of the Infanta's father, King Manuel. "Who, then, was the king your father ? Perchance a tyrant, like Phalaris, or Dionysius of Syracuse ?[20] Certainly not. But he was that man in whose heart burned always such zeal for the Faith, that with great expense to his exchequer, with heavy casualties among his compatriots, with great moil and toil in his body and spirit, he caused the precious blood of Christ to be worshipped where that of brute beasts had been sacrificed. And this at such a far distance from his realms and kingdoms as he himself was close to the glory which he deserved on this account; unfurling banners, storming cities, and subjugating kingdoms in regions never reached by the victorious Alexander and the great Hercules, whose exploits so astonished the Ancients; finding new stars, navigating unknown seas, revealing the ignorance of the old philosophers, whom the world regarded as masters of hidden truths".[21]

Barros then goes on to extol the geographical discoveries made by plain Portuguese pilots with their practical knowledge and navigational skills, gained on the deck of a ship. Their charts, he says, were much more accurate and far-reaching than the maps compiled by the illustrious Ptolemey, "just as if they had studied in some university and as if he had not done so in Athens, where he spent his life". Barros rounds off this particular piece of "triumphalism" with a list of Italian humanists, who, he claims, celebrated and publicised the overseas conquests of King Manuel. They included "Policiano, Filippo, Beroaldo, Blósio, Paládio, Piério, Casálio, and others who in prose and verse spread throughout the world these triumphs of the king your father".[22]

This panegyric, addressed as it was to a "bluestocking" princess, gave Barros the opportunity to recall some of the famous heroines and erudite women of Antiquity and of the Old Testament. His heterogeneous list includes, to name only a few of the many he cites : Judith, who slew Holofernes; Queen Esther, who saved the Israelites from the wrath of King Artaxerxes; the wife and the daughters of Pythagoras, "who clarified the obscure sayings of their husband and father"; Saint Catherine of Alexandria, who confounded many heathen philosophers in public arguments; Mary, the sister of Moses; Sappho, "inventress of these verses";[23] Cornelia, mother and teacher of the eloquent Gracchi brothers; Aspasia, mistress of Pericles and famous for her intellectual attainments, "from whom even Socrates, wisest of mortals, learnt something"; the Queen called Candace of Meroe in Upper Nubia, praised by the Jewish historian Josephus and mentioned in the Acts of the Apostles; the Queen of Sheba, "who went on such a lengthy journey to hear the wisdom of Solomon, and who will lead the twelve tribes of Israel on the day of the wrath of the Lord". He also threw in various Amazons for good measure, including Dido of Carthage and Joan of Arc, "La Pucelle de France".

In his feminist flights of fancy, Barros asks rhetorically what man could equal Queen Cleopatra of Egypt in knowledge and in courage ? Lucrece and Dido are praised for having preferred to die by their own hands rather than to live dishonoured. More pertinently, perhaps, Barros recalls that Christ our Redeemer was "accused by men, sold by men, crucified by men, forsworn by men, and deserted by men. Only the women accompanied Him to the cross and to the tomb". Was it not, he asks, Mary Magdalene who was the first person to whom the risen Christ appeared ? And did not the wife of Pilate, though a gentile, try to persuade her husband not to pass a death-sentence on Him ?

Warming to his theme, Barros waxes eloquent over the conduct and courage of the females among the early Christian martyrs. "How many bodily mutilations, how many severed heads, how many roasted corpses of women, does not the Holy Mother Church celebrate each year ?" The courage of the 11,000 virgins, not one of whom renounced her faith under threat of torture, is contrasted favourably with the cowardice of the male disciples, who one and all abandoned Christ in the Garden of Gethsemane. Climaxing his praise of classical and of Christian female paragons, Barros adds that he could quote, if necessary, many more exemplars of the great extent to which women "flourished in every branch of letters, in arms, in ruling kingdoms, in founding cities, in working miracles, in constancy in the faith, and in enduring martyrdoms therefor; in the virtues of chastity, piety, and mercy, as well as in all the others, in which they not only equalled men but often surpassed them".[24]

After this high-flown peroration, the panegyric concludes on a more material note, with a politely veiled appeal to the princess that she and her kingly half-brother should favour and reward "these your people and vassals" (*este seu povo e vassalos*), who in their turn will ever pray for her long life and happiness.

(c) *Evangelical Dialogue Concerning the Articles of the Faith against the Talmud of the Jews* (c. *1543*)

Towards the end of his panegyric in honour of the Infanta Dona Maria, João de Barros expressed the hope that the Portuguese royal family might yet produce a prince who would roll back the tide of heresy in Europe and extend the true faith there; as her father and her half-brother had done in Asia, Africa, and America. There was, he opined, some hope of this coming to pass; for the royal family had already produced so saintly a Religious as another of her half-brothers, the Infante Dom Henrique, "whose manners, holy virtue and most pure life, represent in our days the great Gregory, Basil, or Augustine. And then there would no longer be Lutherans in our time; Bohemia would render obedience to the sovereign pontiff; Greece, with all its mixture of Jacobite, Georgian, Armenian and Abyssinian sects, would be reconciled to the faith; and there would be an end to as many kinds of heresies as there are at present in the world".[25]

Barros' hopes regarding the reunion of Christendom were to be disappointed; but his eulogistic reference to the Infante Dom Henrique, who was created successively Inquisitor-General of Portugal (1539), Archbishop of Evora (1540), and Cardinal in 1545, was not fortuitous. Some two years earlier, Barros had dedicated to the Archbishop-Inquisitor, as he then was, a polemical treatise directed against the beliefs held (or commonly thought to be held) by Jews and crypto-Jews. In the undated preface to this *Evangelical Dialogue concerning the Articles of the Faith against the Talmud of the Jews*, Barros explains that he has written this work, like a vigilant sheep-dog guarding the fold presided over by Dom Henrique, to give the alarm against "some wolves of Talmudists", whom he had heard and seen making anti-Christian comments during the celebration of the first three *autos-da-fé* recently held at Lisbon.[26] As Révah pointed out in his masterly introduction to the definitive edition of the *Diálogo Evangélico*, this polemical work must have been compiled soon after the third *auto-da-fé* had been celebrated in November, 1542. Since the text of the work gives indications of having been composed in rather a hurry, it was probably finished fairly early in the year 1543.

Révah further notes that the date of the composition of the manuscript helps to clarify two of the principal objectives of João de Barros in writing it. On the one hand, the *Dialogue* is obviously intended to demonstrate the truth of Christianity to hostile Jews and to doubting or hesitant New-Christians. As such, it is typical of the polemical anti-Jewish literature of the period. On the other hand, Barros was more specifically concerned with two contemporary phenomena among the Portuguese "New Christians" : the development of Messianism, as evidenced by the recent appearance of several impostors claiming to be the Messiah, and the efforts of the crypto-Jews to emigrate to other countries where they could practise their ancestral faiths in freedom, and especially to the relatively tolerant Turkish empire.[27]

The *Dialogue* opens with two travellers meeting at a parting of the ways, with the right-hand road leading to Rome and the left to Turkey. One traveller personifies the Gospel (*Evangelho*) and the other the *Talmud.* Having revealed their identity to each other, and the *Talmud* having explained that he is bound for Venice and thence to Turkey, *Gospel* retorts : "How glad I am to find you here, in a place where you cannot avoid listening to me, so that I can warn you not to continue on your way to Turkey, but to follow that which is the real way and the Truth (John. xiv, 6). If you and your followers take this road, you will not imperil soul and life". Otherwise, *Talmud* may meet with the same fate as some of those miscreants "who follow your perverse doctrine" recently did.

Talmud then asks how these unfortunates had lost their lives and why he had been the cause thereof. *Gospel* replies that *Talmud* is to blame for having led astray by his lies and deceits the New-Christians who had been accounted as true converts to Christianity. But "my daughter, the Holy Inquisition, who now resides in Portugal", has taken cognizance of this problem. Like a merciful queen, she is anxious peacefully to reconcile these sinners with the Church, through the intermediary of the merciful Infante Dom Henrique, Archbishop of Evora. But his brother, King John III, seeing how some of the accused obstinately persisted in their perverse beliefs, he, "as captain and defender of the Faith, ordered his ministers of justice to burn them to ashes, so that there should be no memory left of their burial-place". *Talmud* retorts : "The torment of death cannot touch such as these. For the souls of the just (says the Scripture) are in the hands of God. And the martyrdom of my people is nothing new to me, above all in Spain, where they have always used such cruelty with them. And finally, however much fire there may be, they are a people blessed of God. He will always multiply them".[28]

João de Barros, by depicting the two protagonists as *Gospel* and *Talmud*, has evidently tried to give his polemical work the structure of a dispute between two religions rather than between two individuals or two races. Despite his defence of the Inquisition, natural enough under the circumstances, the tone adopted by Barros throughout this *Dialogue* is, on the whole, one of relative moderation. There is certainly not such a violent and sweeping attack on the Jewish values of the Old Testament as there was in the *Ropica Pnefma*. In this *Evangelical Dialogue*, Barros tries to prove the superiority of Christianity over Judaism by arguments drawn from the Old and New Testaments, from the Apocalypse and from various post-Biblical Jewish texts and Rabbinical writings. However, as Révah has conclusively shown, João de Barros' knowledge of the *Talmud* was both fragmentary and inaccurate, apart from being at second or third hand. He knew no Hebrew, and when he wrote *Ropica Pnefma* in 1531, he thought that the *Talmud* was a canonical book for Muslims as well as for Jews. Twelve years later, his grasp of Judaism was still not much better. In the *Evangelical Dialogue*, he relies very heavily on four standard polemical anti-Jewish works, embodying many passages of them wholesale, usually without acknowledgement.[29]

The only one of these four works to which he makes specific acknowledgement is a Latin dialogue by Pedro Alfonso, a Spanish Jew who was baptised in 1106, and who made use of some arguments taken from the *Cabala* and the *Midrash*. Some observations on the Cabala are also taken from Johann Reuchlin (1455-1522), *De Cabala, seu symbolica receptione*, one of the most widely read and quoted books of its kind in the sixteenth century, and one which Barros plundered freely.[30] His two other principal sources were Pietro Galatino, *Opus toti Christianae Reipublicae maxime utile, de arcanis catholicae veritatis, contra obstinatissimam Judaeorum nostrae tempestatis perfidiam : ex Talmud, aliisque hebraicis libris nuper excerptum et quadruplici linguarum genere elegant congestum* (Bari, 1516) and H. Fino, *In Judaeos Flagellum* (Venice, 1538). Révah observes that Barros could not have relied on worse informants than these two last-named; the first on account of his dishonesty, and the second on account of his ignorance. The accuracy of the works of Pedro Alfonso and J. Reuchlin also left a good deal to be desired.[31]

Since Barros relied heavily on such misleading sources, and since his own knowledge of Hebrew was *nil*, there is no point in my trying to analyse and evaluate in detail the *Diálogo Evangelico*, especially since my own competence in this field is even less than that of João de Barros. Fortunately, as the reader will undoubtedly have gathered by now, this task has been done once for all by the late Professor I.S. Révah, to whose eruditely annotated edition of 1950 the interested reader is referred.

It only remains to conjecture why this work was never published, despite the fact that it was dedicated to the Archbishop-Inquisitor and that Barros was then high in the favour of the king and the royal family. Here again, Professor Révah has supplied the most likely answer. The atmosphere of 1543 was rather different from that when *Ropica Pnefma* was published. With the establishment of the Portuguese branch of the Inquisition, and the tightening of the censorship, Dom Henrique and his ecclesiastical advisers doubtless felt that it would be awkward to discuss such dangerous ideas so frankly, even if the object of the work in question was to refute them. Two other polemical and anti-Judaical works, both of which were dedicated to Dom Henrique about the same time, were also either suppressed or drastically revised before publication, for the same reason. These were the *Espelho de Christãos Novos e Convertidos* (*Mirror of the New Christians and Converts*), of Francisco Machado in 1541, and the *Inquisiçam e segredos da Fé, contra a obstinada perfidia dos Judeus* (*Inquisition and secrets of the Faith, against the obstinate perfidy of the Jews*) by Diogo de Sá.[32] I may add that in Barros' *Evangelical Dialogue*, *Talmud* is not finally convinced by Gospel's arguments, and that many of the passages in which the former vigorously denies the divinity of Christ, the validity of the Resurrection, etcetera, may well have seemed more convincing to potential New Christian readers than were *Gospel's* often longwinded and laboured refutations.[33]

However that may have been, the suppression of the *Evangelical Dialogue* was very effective and the manuscript lay neglected at Evora for over two centuries. Manuel Severim de Faria does not mention it in his *Life* of 1624, nor does Diogo Barbosa Machado in his massive *Bibliotheca Lusitana, Historica, Critica, e Chronologica* (5 vols., Lisboa, 1741-59), although the latter records the similar works of Francisco Machado and Diogo de Sá. Only in 1810 was its existence divulged; but it remained unused until 1912, and unpublished (save for an extract) until Professor Révah's definitive edition of 1950. Admittedly, the *Evangelical Dialogue* does its author no great credit from either a theological or a literary viewpoint. But, as Professor Révah has observed, if we cannot include João de Barros among the Portuguese scholars of Hebrew, this abortive polemical work reflects the great interest which he always shewed in the Jewish problem of his day and generation.

NOTES

1. "Não sem causa, muito alto e muito poderoso Rei e Senhor, costumavam nos tempos antigos louvar os excelentes homens em sua presença, por que dando louvor justo e manifesto ao grande merecimento das pessoas, assi os presentes, como os que viessem depois, tomassem exemplo e fizessem tais obras com que merecessem o mesmo louvor" (p. 1 of the Clássicos Sá da Costa edition by M. Rodrigues Lapa, *João de Barros. Panegiricos, 2a* ed., Lisboa, 1943). All my citations and references below are made to this edition, which is vastly superior to the faulty first edition of 1740.
2. *Panegíricos* (ed. 1943), pp. 1-2.
3. *Panegíricos* (ed. 1943), pp. 1-2.
4. Compare the declaration of Damião de Góis to the Inquisitors in 1571 : "Depois que vim a Portugal no ano de 1533. . . por El-Rei que santa glória haja saber que vira eu já Erasmo Roterodamo e que éramos amigos, me perguntou se o poderia eu fazer vir a este reino para se dele servir em Coimbra, onde já tinha ordenado de fazer os estudos que fez, ao que lhe respondi o que me disso parecia" (*apud* J.S. da Silva Dias, *A Pólitica Cultural da época de D. João III*, Vol. I, p. 382, and Raul Rego, *O Processo de Damião de Goes na Inquistção*, Lisboa, n.d., p. 139). Cf. also Elisabeth Feist Hirsch, *Damião, de Góis* (1967), p. 70.
5. *Panegíricos* (ed. 1943), pp. 22, 50, 64, 73, 75, 95-97, 106, 145.
6. *Vossa Alteza*, "Your Highness", was the title usually given to Portuguese kings at this period, *Vossa Magestade*, "Your Majesty", coming into general use some years later. Cf. Martin de Albuquerque, *O Poder Politico no Renascimento Portugues* (Lisboa, 1968), pp. 358-61.
7. *Panegíricos* (ed. 1943), pp. 23-24.
8. *Panegíricos* (ed. 1943), p. 26. For other exaltations of Portuguese militant and missionary expansion in Asia see *op.cit.*, pp. 38-39, 124-25.
9. King John III reminded the French monarch in January 1534 that if the Portuguese had taken six or seven French ships by way of reprisal, the French had taken some 350 sail from the Portuguese. Cf. Fr. Luís de Sousa, O.P., *Anais de D. João III* (ed. M. Rodrigues Lapa), Vol. II, p. 237, Lisboa, 1954; Alfredo Pimenta, *Dom João III* (Porto, 1936), pp. 108-27, and the sources there quoted.
10. *Panegíricos* (ed. 1943), pp. 121, 137-38, *inter alia*.
11. What an English Protestant clergyman wrote of King Pedro II in 1699 could be applied with equal truth to King Manuel I and King John III : "He hath so great an aversion to wine, that he doth not only refrain from it himself, but obliges all about him to a like abstinence. Nor doth he find it difficult to make himself obeyed in this point. . . People of this country, persons of quality more especially, and indeed, all that have the least regard to their credit,

being very shy of drinking wine" (John Colbatch, *Account of the Court of Portugal*, 1699, pp. 3-5).

12. " . . . Levando ele só má vida, com que nós todos vivamos descançados" (*Panegíricos*, ed. 1943, p. 116).
13. ". . . este mesmo o faz cuidar novas maneiras e novas invencoes d'estudos gerais, por onde as ciências em seu reino não menos cresçam e vão adiante, que as outras virtudes" (*op. et loc. cit.*) cf. above.
14. *Panegíricos*, p. 75.
15. *Panegíricos*, pp. 133-35. The reference is to the defeat and capture of Francis I of France at the battle of Pavia (24 Feb. 1525) by the Spaniards and Imperialists.
16. British Museum, Landsdowne Mss. 255, fl. 444. Undated and unsigned, but evidently written shortly after the death of John III in 1557.
17. First published by Manuel Severim de Faria in his posthumous *Notícias de Portugal* (Lisboa, 1655), and edited by M. Rodrigues Lapa in *Panegíricos* (1943) pp. 161-219. For Viseu as the presumed birthplace of João de Barros, see I.S. Révah (1958), p. 67 and *Ibidem* (1962), p. 588, note (32); Alexandre de Lucena e Vale, "No quarto centenário de João de Barros", in *Anais da Academia Portuguesa da História*, II Série, Vol. 19 (1970), pp. 201-223.
18. Carolina Michaelis de Vasconcelos, *A Infanta Dona Maria de Portugal e as suas damas* (Lisboa, 1902) is still the standard biography of this princess.
19. *Panegíricos* (ed. 1943), pp. 165-66, Cf. I.S. Révah (1958), p. 67, and *Ibidem*, (1962), pp. 588-89.
20. Phalaris, a 6th-century tyrant of Acragas (Agrigento) in Sicily, who was notorious for his cruelty, mentioned by Barros (rather inaccurately) in the *Ropica Pnefma*. Cf. ch. 3 (note 12). Dionysius I, Tyrant of Sicily (c. 430-367 B.C.) is presumably the one intended here, although his son, Dionysius II, was tyrant from 367 until his expulsion in 343 B.C.
21. *Navegando mares não conhecidos* (*Panegíricos*, ed. 1943, p. 161), an anticipation of Camoes' more famous line *Por mares nunca de antes navegados* (*Lusíadas I*, 1, line 3).
22. Of the Italian humanists cited in this passage, the first mentioned is Camillo Porzio, one of the chief papal orators under Pope Leo X, with a salary of 150 gold florins. His *Camilli Porcii Ro. in Laudem Emanuellis Lusitaniae regis Leoni X Pontifici Max dicta oratio*, was reprinted in a limited facsimile edition by Eugenio de Canto (Lisboa, 1902). He was also one of the contributors of Latin verses printed at the end of the Oration of Obedience delivered by Diogo Pacheco to Pope Leo X in 1514 and printed at Rome in the same year. He should not be confused with his better known homonym, the Neapolitan historian (1526-1580). Angelo Poliziano (1454-94) had offered to write a eulogistic account in Latin or in

Greek of the Portuguese discoveries during the reign of King John II, but nothing seems to have come of it. Filippo Beroaldo is probably the younger (1472-1518) of the two Italian humanists of that name. In his *Carmina* (posthumous edition, 1530), he lauded the Portuguese conquests in Asia, urging that the Christian princes should stop fighting among themselves and unite in a crusade against the Turks, as preached by Pope Leo X. He was made Librarian of the Vatican in 1516. Blosio Palladio (Palladius Blosius) erroneously split into two individuals by the insertion of a comma in the pointed text, received Roman citizenship in 1516. He was head of the Roman Academy, which met in his villa by the Tiber, and died in 1550. Pierio Valerianus (1477-1560) was a prolific humanist writer, patronised by Popes Julian II and Leo X. Casalio is presumably Gianbattista Casalio, physician and apostolic notary, who became Bishop of Belluno in 1527.

Elsewhere in this panegyric, Barros mentions (p. 192 of the 1943 text) the following humanists of an earlier period who were patronized by King Alfonso V (1396-1458) of Aragon and of Naples, which he made into the cultural capital of Italy : Bartolomeo Fazio (1400-1457), who taught at Florence and Genoa before entering the service of King Alfonso at Naples. Fazio had a lengthy polemic with Lorenzo Valla, who is also cited approvingly by Barros. Valla (1407-1457) was probably the greatest representative of the critical and innovative spirit of Italian humanism. His work in the fields of philology, philosophy and historiography profoundly influenced Erasmus. Giovanni Aurispa (c. 1376-1459) was a famous and gifted humanist of Sicilian origin. Antonio Panormita (Panormitano) whose real name was Antonio Becadelli (1394-1471), was chiefly known for his *Hermophroditus*, a collection of epigrams, amorous, satirical and eulogistic (1425).

Barros' knowledge of the works of these humanists and his connections with others, such as Paolo Giovio (1483-1552) have not yet been investigated. But this is a task for someone with the qualifications of Dr. J.V. de Pina Martins, Fr. Francisco Leite de Faria, O.F.M. Cap., or Dr. Luis de Matos, and not for one who has "little Latin and less Greek". In identifying them, I have relied chiefly on Mario Emilio Cosanza, *Biographical and Bibliographical Dictionary of the Italian Humanists and of the World of Classical Scholarship in Italy, 1300-1800* (6 vols., G.K. Hall & Co., Boston, Mass., 1962-67).

23. Sappho (born *c.* 612 B.C.), Greek lyric poetess of Mytilene in Lesbos, wrote in a variety of metres including the "Sapphic" which was copied by Horace.

24. *Panegiricos* (1943) pp. 206-18, for Barros' pro-feminist peroration, which should not be taken too seriously, but is interesting nonetheless.

25. *Panegíricos* (1943), pp. 218-19. The Infante Dom Henrique is here compared with Pope St. Gregory the Great (*c.* 540-604), St. Basil (329-79), one of the Fathers of the Greek Church, and St. Augustine (354-430), the most celebrated Father of the Latin Church.
26. "E porque em tres autos da Santa Inquisicam que per mandado de V.A. em Lisboa sam feitos (sobre a vegia da grege evangelica), vi e ouvi alguns lobos talmudistas que perseguem o pegulhal eleito" (*Diálogo Evangélico sobre os artigos da Fé contra o Talmud dos Judeus. Manuscrito inédito de João de Barros, o autor das Décadas* (ed. I.S. Révah, Lisboa, 1950, p. 1).
27. *Diálogo* (ed. Révah), pp. 1xxiii-1xxiv.
28. *Diálogo* (ed. Révah), pp. 4-5. "Above all in Spain" (*principalmente em Espanha*) refers, of course, to the Iberian kingdoms of Spain and Portugal.
29. *Diálogo* (ed. Révah), pp. 1xxvi-1xxxix, pp. 129-54, for a detailed confrontation of the relevant texts with that of the *Diálogo*.
30. *Diálogo* (ed. Révah), p. 1xxix for the full title of *Petri Alphonsi ex Judaeo christiani Dialogi lectu dignissimi*. Kabbala, Cabella, or Cabala, the theosophy or mystic philosophy of the Hebrew religion, which developed mainly after the beginning of the 10th century. A Christian form of the Cabala had a considerable vogue in the 15th-16th centuries, Johann Reuchlin being one of its exponents.
31. *Diálogo* (ed. Révah), pp. 1xxvi-1xxxix.
32. *Diálogo* (ed. Révah), pp. 1xix-1xvii, 1xxxix, for the works of Francisco Machado a sixteenth-century Cistercian monk of Alcobaça, and Diogo de Sá who became a distinguished jurisconsult in Portugal after serving twelve years as a frontier-fighter (*fronteiro*) in India.
33. *Diálogo* (ed. Révah), pp. 47, 56, 63-64, 88, for typical instances.

5

GRAMMATICAL AND DIDACTIC WORKS

In the years 1539-40, while he was still busily engaged on writing his *Decades*, and with a full-time job as Factor of the India and Guinea Houses, João de Barros published a remarkable series of pedagogical and didactic works. Destined primarily for the moral and educational instruction of children and adolescents, some of them were also, as he himself remarked, suitable for the instruction of Asian and African neophytes, who wanted to learn Portuguese and the basic elements of the Christian religion. Barros had originally envisaged publishing them together, under the general title of *Grammatica da Lingua Portuguesa com os mandamentos da Santa Madre Igreja* (*Grammar of the Portuguese Language with the Commandments of Holy Mother Church*). However, the publishers decided to issue the work in separate parts, presumably with the idea of helping sales; so we may consider them here in the chronological order in which they appeared.

(a) *Grammar of the Portuguese Language with the Commandments of Holy Mother Church*

The general title of the series was (confusingly) used for this relatively small first part, of which the colophon reads : "To the praise of God and of the glorious Virgin Mary, this primer (*Cartinha*) with the precepts and commandments of Holy Mother Church, and with the mysteries of the mass, and the responsories thereof, was finished printing in the very noble and always loyal city of Lisbon, by the authority of the holy Inquisition, in the house of Luis Rodriguez, bookseller to our Lord the King, with his royal privilege on the 20 December in the year 1539".[1]

This was one of the first works in Portugal to be published

with the licence of the Inquisition after the original manuscript had been submitted to that body for censorship and clearance. It was dedicated to the young Prince Philip,[2] with a preface addressed to him, which was clearly intended to cover the series as a whole. In the event, this preface only appeared in this first part, which, understandably enough, is nearly always cited by the title of *Primer* (*Cartinha, Cartilha*) which was given it in the colophon. We retain this usage here, since this first part is a catechism-primer and not a grammar, as the title-page erroneously implies.

In the dedicatory-preface addressed to Prince Philip, Barros emphasises that the work as a whole is intended not only for him, but for the converts gained by the expansion of the Faith under Portuguese auspices overseas. "Of which work we now have a divine example in the conversion of 57,000 souls in the land of Malabar, where Saint Thomas with such toil and martyrdom passed from this life to celestial glory.[3] Fired by the zeal to learn our language, four of their chief men came here this year, for they could learn to speak it more easily in these kingdoms than they could at home; and through our language they can also learn the precepts of the religion in which they hope to end. The King, your father, ever zealous for the Faith, ordered them to be maintained in the monastery of St. Eloi of this city, so that they can study there with the other Ethiopians from the Congo, from whom we have already formed here Bishops and theologians—certainly something very new in the Church of God, even though it is prophesied in Psalm 71".[4]

Barros goes on to explain that to help these Asians and Africans learning Portuguese, as well as for the benefit of the young prince and his child compatriots, he has compiled this primer, catechism, and grammar, followed by a couple of dialogues, one in praise of the Portuguese language and the other a moral treatise on vice and virtue. As noted above, the printer-publisher split these up into four separate works, the contents of the first part, published in December 1539, being as follows :

Pictorial representation of the alphabet and rules for spelling and reading.

"Our Father" and "Hail Mary" in Latin and Portuguese.
The Creed in Latin and Portuguese.
Explanation of the Creed.
Salve Regina in Latin and Portuguese.
The Ten Commandments of the Law and the Five of the Church.
The Seven Sacraments of the Church.
The Fourteen Works of Mercy (Seven Corporal and Seven Spiritual).
The Seven Theological and the Seven Moral Virtues.
The Twelve fruits of the Holy Spirit.
The Three enemies of the soul and the five senses against them.
The Seven Mortal Sins and the Seven Virtues against them.
Grace at Table, and other graces.
Treatise on the mass.
The Gospel of St. John, ch. I. verses i-xi.
The symbol of *Quicumque vult.*
The prayers of the Just Judge and *Obsecio Te domina.*
Prayer to the Host, and prayer to the chalice.
Monthly Fast and Feast-Days.
Prayer to the Guardian Angel.
How to calculate the four Ember weeks.

It will be seen that the *Cartinha* comprised a preliminary section (pp. 1-15) on the alphabet and rules of spelling, followed by a selection of religious texts (pp. 16-54), forming a catechism in which the pupil could practise reading at the same time as imbibing Roman Catholic doctrine. This was the structure of all the known Protuguese *cartinhas* of the 16th century, both before and after that of Barros, with insignificant variations. There is no influence of the Counter-Reformation to be discerned here, since the contents are clearly of medieval origin. However, this 1539 *Cartinha* of João de Barros is noticeably superior to all the others from a didactic and pedagogic viewpoint. His inclusion of an illustrated *a b c*, each letter having a pictorial explanation, such as a tree (*arvore*) for A, a ship (*náo*) for N, an eye (*olho*) for O, a fox (*raposa*) for R, etc., is especially noteworthy. This innovation would seem to make Barros a precursor of J.A. Comenius, the noted Czech theologian and educational reformer (1592-1670), particulary since Barros' pioneer effort is in some ways better structured and more efficient.[5]

Apart from the illustrated *a b c*, his catechism was taken over by St. Francis Xavier and adapted for use in the world-wide missions of the Society of Jesus. As such, its influence was lasting and enormous. Barros' *Cartinha* does not seem to have been so popular in his own country as was a less valuable one by Fr. Jõao Soares (1507-1572), a rather shady if talented ecclesiastic, who became tutor to the royal children, an Inquisitor, and Bishop of Coimbra. The *Cartinha* of Fr. João Soares had four editions in the second half of the sixteenth century (and possibly one before 1550), whereas the *Cartinha* of João de Barros was not reprinted textually until 1785.

The *Catechism* of Barros was however, translated into Tamil by Thomé da Cruz, one of the four Malabar (Parava) converts to whom Barros alludes in his preface. It was published with an interlinear Tamil and Portuguese text at Lisbon early in 1554. Presumably, virtually all of the copies were sent to India. At any rate, it is now excessively rare, only one recorded copy having so far been traced.[6]

(b) *Grammar of the Portuguese Language* (*Grammatica da Lingua Portuguesa*) *1540.*

Although published with the same title as the preceding piece, this was the *Grammar*, properly speaking, to which the *Cartinha* (also confusingly entitled *Grammatica*, as we have seen) was the necessary preliminary. There is no colophon, but the title-page is dated 1540. It must have been printed early in January of that year, since the *Dialogue of Sinful Shame*, which forms the third part of this series, was printed on the 12 January 1540 (p. 90 below). This *Dialogue* is often cited as if it was a completely separate item from the *Grammar*; but the pagination of the original edition is continuous and it was clearly intended as an integral if complementary portion of the larger work.

This was not the first published Grammar of Portuguese. Barros had been "pipped at the post", so to speak, by Fernando (or Fernão) Oliveira, a singularly outspoken and indeed maverick priest, who published the pioneer Portuguese grammar in 1536.[7] Oliveira had at one time been tutor to some of the sons of João de Barros, and it has been claimed that he plagiarised the latter's work when it was still in manuscript, but the differences between the two grammars are greater than their points of resemblance. In any event, the two scholars must obviously have had some conversations with each other on this and other matters of mutual interest. João de Barros does not mention Fernando Oliveira in his own *Grammar*, but the latter does allude to "the very noble João de Barros" (*o mui nobre João de Barros*) in his prior version of 1536.

Each of them, incidentally, was careful to claim priority for his own work, Barros, writing in the third person, and to illustrate a grammatical rule, states explicitly : "João de Barros was the first to treat of our language in a methodical way : and the memory of his son, António, who took it to our lord the prince, will not be forgotten." Here the name of João de Barros stands without an article; and that of António is governed by the preposition 'of'. Fernando Oliveira claimed equally emphatically and explicitly that he wrote his own *Grammar* "without having any other example before me". Perhaps the explanation is that both works were ready about the same time, since Phince Philip, to whom Barros' Grammar was dedicated, died in 1536, the same year in which Oliveira's work was published. Barros can hardly have failed to have known of its existence; but he evidently let his claim to priority stand, just as he did not drop the dedication to the dead prince when he published his *Grammatica* four years later.

Both Barros and Oliveira had been preceded in the Iberian world by the Castilian Grammar (*Grammatica Castellana*) of the famous Spanish humanist, António de Nebrija, published at Salamanca in 1492, the year of the reconquest of Granada and the discovery of America. A comparison of the two pioneer Portuguese grammars shows that of Oliveira to be more original in some ways, but that of Barros, modelled on the standard Latin grammars of the period, to be more systematic and comprehensive. Both were certainly indebted to some extent to Nebrija, but while Barros' Grammar can be considered as the Portuguese equivalent of the Castilian work, it is certainly not a slavish adaptation of it and there are many points of difference. There is a fundamental divergence in their conception of what a grammar should be. As Maria Leonor Carvalhão Buescu has written: "Nebrija is the speculative grammarian, the scientist of the language. Barros is the teacher and the pedagogue", and his work was aimed at a less exigent audience. Barros included in his grammar a section on orthography, in which he advocated an original method of spelling and accentuation; but this innovation does not seem to have had any influence on contemporaries or on posterity.[8]

Vernacular grammars were still a novelty in the first-half of the sixteenth century, and one of the declared objects of João de Barros was to inculcate the teaching of Portuguese grammar before the pupil went on to tackle Latin. Oliveira evidently thought the same; but neither of them seem to have been successful in replacing the standard Latin grammars which were used as textbooks in the schools and colleges at what would now be called the secondary level.[9] Neither of them was reprinted for centuries—Barros for the first time in 1795, and Oliveira in 1871. Not more than two or three copies of the respective original editions have survived, and contemporary references to them are conspicuous by their absence.

It is true that Pedro de Magalhães de Gandavo utilised the *Grammar* of João de Barros in his own *Rules for teaching how to write and spell the Portuguese language, with a complementary dialogue in defence of the said language* (*Regras que ensinam a maneira de escrever a ortografia da lingua Portuguesa, com hum Dialogo que se segue em defensam da mesma lingua*), which had three editions between 1574 and 1591. But Gandavo's work was likewise soon relegated to oblivion. Severim de Faria, writing in 1624, still mentions it, but he did not realise that Barros had been preceded by Oliveira. We know that Latin grammatical compendia retained their overwhelming priority, if not their absolute monopoly, in all Portuguese educational establishments, whether clerical or lay, until the Pombaline reforms, which were, in part at least, inspired by the revolutionary *Verdadeiro Método de*

Estudar (*True Method of Studying*) published by António Verney in 1746.[10]

Professor A.J. Saraiva has suggested that these two pioneer sixteenth century grammars, as well as the *Cartinha* of Barros, were primarily intended for the instruction of the Asian and African subjects of the Portuguese Empire. This seems to me to be a misapprehension. Their primary purpose —unsuccessful in the long run, as we have seen—was to foster the teaching of the vernacular in the homeland. Barros stated categorically in his *Dialogue in praise of our language*, to which we must now turn our attention, that his aim in dedicating this whole pedagogical series of 1539-40 to the young Prince Philip was that he (or, in fact, the Crown) should recommend it as a textbook for use in schools, if it were found to be satisfactory.[11]

Both Barros and Oliveira agreed with António de Nebrija that a conquering power was fully justified in imposing the use of its language on subject peoples, just as the Greeks and the Romans had done in the days of their respective imperial grandeur. At the end of a peroration extolling the Romans for their linguistic imperialism, Barros adds with prophetic foresight : "All monarchies perished sooner or later with the inevitable changes of time and of human fortune; however, the Latin language left this imprint of its empire which will last for all time. The Portuguese arms and commemorative pillars (*padrões*) placed in Africa and in Asia, and in so many thousand islands beyond the three continents of the world, are material things, and Time may destroy them. But Time will not destroy the religion, the customs, and the language which the Portuguese have implanted in these lands". He went on to boast in this dialogue with his son : "Certainly there is no glory that can be compared to the fact that the Ethiopian, Persian, and Indian children on the near and the far side of the Ganges, in their own lands and in the precincts of their temples and pagodas, are now learning our language from this our grammar, in which they can be indoctrinated in the precepts of our faith which are contained therein".[12]

Like other Romance humanists, Barros proved to his own satisfaction that his native tongue was the closest of all to

Latin, and thus inherently superior to the others. He rejected the widely-held belief that Portuguese was inferior to Castilian, and that Castilian was inferior to Italian or to French. He extolled the majesty, musicality, and gravity of Portuguese; arguing that French and Italian appeared to be languages more suitable for women, whereas Portuguese was the ideal tongue for men. Moreover : "it is a language so pure and chaste that it is inconceivable that a book like *La Celestina* could be written therein. And the writer of comedies, Gil Vicente, who took more liberties with it than anybody else in these kingdoms, never dared to portray a Portuguese *Centurion*, for as the nation would never tolerate it, neither would the language".[13]

For all his pride in Portuguese as the eldest daughter of Latin, Barros was not so obsessed with the superiority of the classical tongue that he approved of borrowing Latin words and terms indiscriminately. Rather than using archaic or unsuitable Latin words and expressions, he advocated employing those which had been naturalised by long usage in the northern province of Minho e Douro, "preservative of Portuguese seed" (*conservador da semente portuguesa*), even if some ignorant people despised such words, "not recognizing the root from which they sprang".

Barros also approved of incorporating various Asian and African words into Portuguese, specifically mentioning *chatinar* (to trade, to peddle), *beniaga*, (merchandise), *lascarim* (soldier, warrior), *çumbaya* (bowing, obeisance), as words which were already naturalised by 1539, and others are to be found scattered throughout his *Decades*.[14] He severely criticised the low standards of many elementary school-teachers, alleging that "in all our noble towns and cities, any ignorant fool with no qualifications can open a school to teach children. Whereas even a cobbler, which is the lowest of all the working-class callings, cannot set up a shop without first being examined for his proficiency. And the worst harm that an unskilful cobbler does is to spoil his own leather and not the customer's material, whereas bad teachers ruin their pupils for the rest of their lives".[15]

Barros insisted on the advantage of the Roman letter as

opposed to the old Gothic script, and he strongly urged that elementary education should begin with the vernacular, "for if you are well-taught in this, you will easily make progress in the others".[16] In short, in this as in several other respects, João de Barros was in advance of his time, which may help to explain why his pedagogical innovations did not obtain wider currency. If they had done so, as Dr. Fernando Castello-Branco points out, Portugal would have been in the van of educational progress in Europe, instead of being left in the rear as she was by the mid-seventeenth century.

(c) *Dialogue of Sinful Shame*

This portion of the series was published a few days after the two former, on the 12 January 1540, according to the colophon. The rather cryptically worded title (which may be translated "Dialogue of Defective Shame" is taken, Barros states, from a little work by Plutarch entitled *De immodica verecundia*. As Severim de Faria noted in 1624, Barros has not followed Plutarch's prototype closely, but taken a strongly moralising line of his own. This essay, cast in the form of a dialogue with his son, António, is a moral treatise destined to implant the fear of the Lord and the beginning of wisdom in his son and other malleable young teenagers. Barros had originally asked his friend, the celebrated Portuguese humanist—and New Christian—António Luís (149?-1565) to write such a treatise for him. This the latter did, publishing it in 1539, under the similar title of *De pudere*.[17] Either Barros was not altogether satisfied with this work, or else he had not seen it before he published his own in the same year.

In the *Dialogue of Sinful Shame*, Barros defines the different types of *Vergonha* (shame, prudery), deriving from three Latin concepts, *pudor*, *verecundia*, *erubescencia*, for which he could find no exact equivalents in Portuguese. This sounds rather odd, for the word *pudor* (shame, modesty), was surely a Portuguese as well as a Latin term by then. *Verecundia* may be rendered into English as bashfulness, shyness, and *erubescencia* as "blushing" or "reddening" with shame or embarrassment. The dialogue is interlarded with frequent citations from scriptural and classical authorities, as was the discussion in *Ropica Pnefma*. Thus St. Thomas, St. Jerome, and St. Paul are cited along with Cicero, Aristotle, Terence, Plutarch, Juvenal, Plato, Socrates, *et al.*, although classical authorities predominate in many passages, as António complains towards the end. There is some discussion of the difference between "shame" and "guilt" but I confess that this little tract defeats me.

Barros also returns to some of the themes which he had discussed in *Ropica Pnefma*. There is a curious, if passing, emphasis on Christian pacifism, where among the "temporal faults" (*defeitos temporaes*) which are denounced as being the works of Satan, are specifically included "conquest, navigation, and commerce" ("*conquistár, navegár, tratar com todalas outras indústrias que Satanás inventou*"). This sounds rather incongruous when we recall that at this very time João de Barros was busily engaged in writing his *Decades*, which were proudly dedicated to celebrating the Portuguese "conquest, navigation, and commerce" in the East. On the other hand, as we have seen above (p. 59), although it may be illogical and incongruous, it is neither surprising nor inexplicable.

Of more interest, is Barros' angry rebuttal of some unnamed critics who had opined that a layman had no business to concern himself with the religious and theological problems which were discussed in *Ropica Pnefma.* These critics considered that matters of this kind should be left to qualified theologians and ecclesiastics. Barros maintains the contrary view, telling his son at one point : "don't think that this concern with Holy Writ is only commended to those who have received doctoral degrees in Paris : the grace conferred by baptism qualifies all of us . . . and granted that I am not one of those called to exercise the doctrinal office, I am one of those called to honour Holy Writ". Barros confirms the validity of the lay apostolate with his usual wealth of citations.

As the dialogue develops, greater emphasis is laid on the Gospel teaching and the words of Christ. Steadfastness, gratitude, and consideration for others are some of the moral values which are inculcated and exemplified. In the last few pages, António requests and receives from his father specific passages from Scripture, which, when memorised, will enable him to resist specific temptations, such as doing an unlawful good turn for a friend or relative, or giving false evidence, or incitement to revenge, etc.

The dialogue concludes with a pious peroration by João de Barros : "Finally, there is no blow which the world, the flesh, or the devil can inflict on you, against which you cannot find defensive and offensive weapons in the Holy Scripture. For this contains majesty, virtue, sanctity, discretion, reproof, love, hate, reward and every other means of triumphing more gloriously than did Hercules over his labours. For eye hath not seen, nor ear heard, neither hate entered into the heart of man, what is in Christ Jesus, who with the Father and the Holy Spirit may live and reign for world without end Amen".[18]

(d) *Dialogue of Moral Precepts with the Practice thereof Organised like a Game*

This dialogue, forming the final part of the educational and pedagogical series, was printed at Lisbon on the 27 March 1540, according to the colophon.[19] The author's name does not appear on the title-page of this first edition, but the text is cast in the form of a dialogue between João de Barros and two of his children, António and Catarina. The father tells the little girl to be particularly attentive to his explanation of the game, since she has got to present and explain it later to the little princess Dona Maria, daughter of King John III, who later married Philip II of Castile (and who is not to be confused with her aunt of the same name, the erudite Infanta Dona Maria).

Elsewhere, Barros states that he had derived this idea of a symbolic game of draughts from the classical precedent of the philosopher, Cebes of Thebes, a friend of Socrates author of the *Pinax* or "Draught's board", an allegory of human life in which a player divests himself of his vices in order to be conducted by the virtues to the citadel of Happiness. Inspired by this classical model, Barros invented a new game of draughts, in which "I summarised the whole of the *Ethics* of Aristotle, which included all the virtues and vices, whether deriving from excess or defect".[20]

The main object of the game being to foster the "Golden mean" in the minds of the players and to avoid too great divergences in either direction, the thirty-six draughts or counters were labelled in the following manner, with those in the centre column representing the ideal :

malice	prudence	simple-mindedness
cruelty	justice	softness
rashness	fortitude	timidity
intemperance	temperance	insensitiveness
prodigality	liberality	avarice
coarseness	magnificence	meanness
presumption	magnanimity	pusilanimity
ambition	modesty	dishonourableness
wrath	equableness	unprovokable
arrogance	truth	dissimulation
flattery	affability	quarrelsomeness
scurrility	graciousness	rusticity

The text of the dialogue contains an explanation of the theory and practice of the game, in which the players had to utter certain moral precepts in Latin whenever they moved their pieces. These precepts Barros had confessedly derived from the *Moralis in Ethicam introductio* of Jacques Lefèvre d'Etaples, probably from the 1528 edition of this popular work, as professor Silva Terra has suggested.

Barros stated in his second *Decade* of 1552 that the little princess was very pleased with this game and often played it with her royal father. He also regretted that it was not so popular outside the royal household, which led him to abandon his original intention of trying out the same method of teaching the *Economy* and *Politics* of Aristotle. Despite his disappointment, there must have been some demand for this edifying—if rather complicated—game, as another edition of this *Dialogue* was published in 1563. This had a slightly different title, which mentioned Barros as the author, and it contained two additional explanatory illustrations. This 1563 edition is nowadays almost as rare as that of 1540; but I cannot say whether this rarity arose from popularity or from neglect.[21]

NOTES

1. Save where otherwise stated, references to the text are to the definitive and annotated reprint edition by Maria Leonor Carvalhão Buescu, *João de Barros. Gramática da Lingua Portuguesa. Cartinha, Gramática, Diálogo em louvor da nossa linguagem a Diálogo da Viciosa Vergonha. Reprodução Fascsimilada. Leitura, Introdução e anotações* (Lisboa, Faculdade de Letras, 1971). Cited hereafter as Carvalhão Buescu.
2. Dom Felipe, third son of King John III, born in 1533, died six years later on the 29 April 1539, so the manuscript must have been ready for the press before this last date. Even so, it is rather odd that the little prince's death was not mentioned by author or publisher in December 1539.
3. For the Malabar Parava and the Congolese converts educated at Santo Elói, the Lisbón monastery of the blue-robed canons of Saints George and John the Evangelist, see George Schurhammer, S.J., *Francis Xavier, his life, his times*, Vol. I, *Europe, 1506-1541* (Rome, 1973), p. 598. Pending the publication of an English translation, now in the press, of the rest of this work, a densely documented discussion of the Apostle St. Thomas and his grave at São Tomé de Meliapur (Milapur), now a suburb of Madras, will be found in G. Schurhammer S.J., *Franz Xaver, Sein Leben und seine Zeit*, II, *Asien, 1541-1552* (1), *Indien und Indonesien, 1541-1547* (Freiburg, 1963), pp. 552-79.
4. Psalm 72 in the Authorized Version.
5. Fernando Castello-Branco, "Portugal Quinhentista visto através das Cartilhas para ensinar a ler", in *Anais da Academia Portuguesa de História*, II Série, Vol. 21 (Lisboa, 1973), pp. 291-315; *Ibidem*, "Cartilhas Quinhentistas para ensinar a ler", in *Boletim Bibliografico e Informativo. Fundacão Calouste Gulbenkian Centro de Investgaçao Pedagógica* No 14 (Lisboa, 1971), pp. 119-52.
6. D. Fernando de Almeida (ed.), *Cartilha em Tamul e Portugues impressa em .1554 por ordem do Rei* (Edicão Facsimile do Museu Nacional de Arqueologia e Etrologia, Lisboa, 1970). Cf. also Américo Cortez Pinto, *Da famosa Arte de Imprimissão* (Lisboa, 1948), pp. 355-66; G. Schurhammer, S.J., and J. Wicki S.J. (eds.), *Epistolae s. Francisci Xaverii aliaque eius scripta, 1535-1552* (2 vols., Rome, 1944-45), Vol. I, pp. 93-116.
7. Also author of an equally rare *Arte de Guerra do Mar* (*Art of War at Sea*) published at Coimbra in 1555. For the agitated life and times (*c.* 1507-*c.* 1581) of this singular ex-Dominican friar and later secular priest see Henrique Lopes de Mendonça *O Padre Fernando Oliveira e a sua obra nautica* (Lisboa, 1898), and the reprint of the 1555 edition with introduction and commentary by Quirino da Fonseca and Alfredo Botelho de Sousa, published by the *Arquivo Histórico da Marinha* (Lisboa, 1937), I have consulted the third edition of his

Grammatica da Lingoagem Portugesa, ed. Rodrigo de Lá Vogueis (1969).

8. For a detailed consideration of Barros' orthographical innovations see M.L. Carvalhão Buescu, *Gramática* (1971). pp. lviii-lxiv.
9. A.J. Saraiva, *História da Cultura em Portugal*, Vol. II, pp. 185-86.
10. António Alberto de Andrade, *Vernei e a Cultura do seu tempo* (Coimbra, 1965) especially, pp. 184-89.
11. "Nem por eu ter dirigido a su Alteza o trabalho que dizes, devo esperar mais que, por me fazer merçê, o mandar examinar : e sendo taes que possam aproveitar aos mininos, mandará que se leam em as escolas" (*apud* Lucians Stegagno Picchio *João de Barros. Diálogo em louvor da nossa linguagem. Lettura critica dell' edizione del 1540 con una introduzone su la questione della lingua in Portogallo*, Modena, 1959, p. 69). Save where otherwise indicated, all my references to this Dialogue are to this edition.
12. *Diálogo* (ed. Stegagno Picchio), pp. 18-19, 85.
13. *Diálogo* (ed. Stegagno Picchio), pp. 79-80, 99-101. *Centurio* was a ruffianly character in *La Celestina*, the popular title of a famous Spanish work, *La Magicomedia de Calisto y Melibea*, the first edition of which appeared in 1499.
14. These and many other Asian terms used by Barros are explained and defined by Sebastião Rodolfo Dalgado, *Glossário Luso-Asiático* (2 vols., Coimbra, 1919-21).
15. *Diálogo* (ed. Stegagno Picchio), pp. 86-87. Complaints about the incompetence and ignorance of elementary-school teachers were common throughout Western Europe in the 16th-17th centuries. For similar criticism of those in the Northern Netherlands—probably the European state with the highest standard of education—see C.R. Boxer, *The Dutch Seaborne Empire, 1600-1800* (London, 1965), pp. 155-57.
16. Anselmo, nt. 1011. The (unreliable) reprint in the 1785 *Compilacao* has now been advantageously replaced by the edition of M.L. Carvalhão Buescu, *Grámatica* (1973), pp. 411-469.
17. Antōnio Luís, nicknamed "The Greek" (*O Grego*), outstanding classical scholar in both Greek and Latin, as well as a famous practising physician, was appointed Professor of Medicine at Coimbra in March 1547. As Professor Révah has observed, the points of contact between João de Barros and António Luís would almost certainly repay further study.
18. Barros' own rendering of the final paragraph is naturally a little different from that of the Authorized Version into which I have turned it for familiarity's sake : "Porque este, nem olho ô vio, nem orelha ouvio, nem subio em coraçám d'algum hómem, o quál está em Cristo Jesu que, com o Pádre e Espírito Santo, vive e reina *in saecula saeculorum*. Amen". (ed. M.L. Carvalhão Buescu, *Gramática*, p. 468.

19. The only two complete extant copies hitherto recorded are in the Municipal Library of Rouen and in the Ajuda Library, Lisbon, respectively. The former is reproduced in photographic facsimile, with a succinct but valuable commentary by Dr. José F. da Silva Terra, to whose courtesy I am indebted for an offprint : "*Dialogo de Preceitos Moraes* de João de Barros" in *Bulletin des Etudes Portugaises*, N.S , Vol. XXX (Lisboa, 1969), pp. 77-87.
20. *Decáda II* (1553), Livro 4, chap. iv. Cebes, a 5th-century B.C., Greek philosopher, friend and pupil of Socrates and one of the interlocutors in Plato's *Phaedo.* His *Pinax* (the picture) is a philosophical explanation of a table symbolically arranged to represent the dangers and vicissitudes of life; but modern scholarship regards the attribution of this work to him as spurious.
21. Cf. Dr. J.F. da Silva Terra's article quoted in note (19) above.

6

THE DECADES OF ASIA

Although so eminent an authority as the late Professor Hernâni Cidade has emphasised that João de Barros deserves as much attention for being a grammarian and a writer who influenced the evolution of the Portuguese language, as he does for being a chronicler and historian of Portuguese expansion, it was in this last capacity that Barros achieved a modest fame in his lifetime and that his work is increasingly consulted and studied nowadays.[1] Nor is this surprising. Whether we regard Portuguese expansion overseas as a civilizing crusade against the barbarous infidel, or as inspired by the mixture of God and Mammon epitomised in the search for "Christians and Spices", or as a prime example of aggressive imperialism and colonial exploitation, the story is one of absorbing interest. For better or for worse, it was the Portuguese who were the colonial pioneers and who set the pattern which their Dutch, English, and French successors adopted and adapted in varying degrees. If there is any truth in the Napoleonic injunction : "Let my son often read and meditate on history, for it is the only true philosophy", the study of the Portuguese "conquest, navigation. and commerce" from Ceuta to Nagasaki may prove enlightening as well as interesting—and it must begin with the *Decades* of João de Barros.

What Barros originally envisaged was a world-history, methodically planned, of which only three (out of four) volumes, dealing primarily with Asia, were published in his lifetime. As he tells us in the first chapter of the first *Decade* he proposed to deal in turn with each of the three interconnected aspects of the title of "Lord of the Conquest, Navigation and Commerce of India, Arabia and Persia" assumed by King Manuel after the return of Vasco da Gama from his pioneer voyage to India in 1497-99. "The First is *Conquest* which deals with warfare; the second is *Navigation,* which corresponds to geography; and the third is *Commerce,* which applies to merchandise". He goes on to explain that the section on *Conquest* will be subdivided into four parts.

"The first part of this *Warfare* we call *Europe,* beginning with the time when the Romans conquered Spain, in which warfare the Portuguese won a great reputation for themselves by their illustrious exploits, and we give a narrative history of subsequent events until the time of the Count Dom Henrique (of Burgundy) and his successors. The second part we call *Africa,* which begins with the taking of Ceuta (in 1415). The third part, which is the one we now have in hand, is called *Asia,* since it treats of the discovery and conquest of the lands and seas of the East, beginning with the time of the Infante Dom Henrique, who was the originator of this Southern (*Austral*) and Oriental warfare. And the fourth will be called Santa Cruz, because this is what we term in our *Geography* the land of Brazil, and because this was the proper name given it by Pedro Alvares Cabral, when he discovered it on his way to India[2]. . . . And of all these four parts dealing with *Warfare,* we have compiled so far in this present year of 1539, forty books comprising four Decades, dealing with Asia, which we now wish to publish as evidence of our work. If God gives us life and the opportunity of so doing, we hope in due time to continue these *Decades* in the same chronological order".

Despite his categorical assertion that the first four *Decades* were ready for the press in 1539, another passage in *Decade* I shows that Barros was still tinkering with the first chapter of the ninth book ten years later. He mentions here that he had received "in the past year of 1548" a sketch of the recently discovered tombstone of St. Thomas the Apostle at Mailapur.[3] There are plenty of similar references in this and in subsequent *Decades* to show that Barros revised and expanded his text as new information became available between 1539 and 1563.

The word *Decada* (Decade) does not appear on the title-page of the first volume, published in June 1552, which reads in translation: *Asia of João de Barros, of the Deeds done by the Portuguese in their Discovery and Conquest of the Seas and Lands of the East*. But as Barros tells us that he modelled his work on the *History* of Livy by devoting a ten-year period to each volume, and as the word *Decada* figures in the title pages of Volumes II-IV, as well as in the running heading to the text of Volume I, the four *Decades* are invariably termed collectively *Decadas da Asia* (*Decades of Asia*). As Professor Donald Lach has observed, the *Decades* may be characterized as a chronicle-narrative organized on geographical lines. Barros never forgot his global overview of Portuguese expansion. Borrowing a metaphor from Professor Niels Steensgaard, we can say that the *Decades*, like an enormous radar screen, reflect the entire scope of Portuguese expansion from the Maranhão to the Moluccas.[4] So much will be clear if we take a brief survey of each volume.

(*a*) *Decade I, 593-1505*

The first *Decade* covers very briefly the historical background to the Discoveries, the work of Prince Henry (inaptly christened "The Navigator" by 19th-century English scholars) and his successors, and the round-voyage of Vasco da Gama (Books 1-4). This preliminary section is followed by a narrative of Portuguese activities in the East from 1500 to 1505 (Books 5-10). Barros is not a first-rate authority on the early Portuguese voyages down the coast of West Africa, since he confessedly relied mainly on Gomes Eanes da Zurara, whose *Chronicle of Guinea* leaves a good deal to be desired.[5]

With the reign of King John II, and still more with that of King Manuel I, the narrative of Barros gains in credibility and reliability, as he had more and better sources at his disposal. Perhaps the most interesting chapters in the first-three books are those describing the building of the castle of São Jorge da Mina in Guinea by Diogo de Azambuja in 1482 (Book III, chapters 1-2), and the relations of the Portuguese with the Jalof kingdom in Senegambia and with the Edo kingdom of Benin (Book III, chapters 4-8, 12).[6] Book IV is entirely devoted to a narrative of the round-voyage of Vasco da Gama, which lasted for almost exactly two years (July 1497-July

1499), but it also includes a short description of Hindustan, "India dentro do Gange" (ch. 7).

Book V deals with the round-voyage of the fleet of Pedro Alvares Cabral (March 1500-June/July 1501). He commanded the first large armada sent to India, and he carried instructions to enforce ruthlessly King Manuel's somewhat premature claim to the overlordship of the Indian Ocean, which had been made immediately after Vasco da Gama's return.[7] Book VI deals with Vasco da Gama's second voyage to India (1502-1504). In the first chapter of this book, Barros gives a very interesting explanation and justification of Portuguese imperialism, which is worth a brief consideration here, since it epitomised a widely held and a staunchly maintained official viewpoint.

"Because (as we have repeated several times) the Supreme Pontiffs had conceded to this kingdom everything which might be discovered between Cape Bojador and the far Oriental shore, which includes the whole of India, islands, seas, ports, fisheries, etc., as listed at length in the papal donations[8] . . . For even though there does exist a common law (*direito comum*) which allows all navigators to sail the seas freely . . .this law applies only to the whole of Europe and its Christian inhabitants, who have been placed within the fold of the Church of Rome by baptism and by faith, and who are also governed by Roman law in their polity. . . But as regards Muslims and Heathens, who are outside the law of Jesus Christ, which is the true law that everyone has to keep under pain of damnation to eternal fire—if these are condemned in their souls, being the principal part of them, their bodies which are animated by those souls cannot plead the privileges of our laws, since the adherents of those creeds are not members of the evangelical congregation, even though they may be our neighbours as rational beings and though they may live to be converted to the true Faith".

This justification of militant Christianity and of aggressive Portuguese expansion may seem a far cry from the pacifist and Erasmian sentiments of the *Ropica Pnefma*; but it is perfectly in tune with the crusading attitude which Barros had previously expressed in *Clarimundo* (p. 44) and in the Panegyrics to King John III and to the Infanta Dona Maria (pp. 71). Some commentators have tied themselves in knots, trying to explain how Barros could harbour such contradictory feelings about war and peace, but I do not see any problem. We do not need psychiatrists to tell us that every human being is a bundle of contradictions, or that patriotism is regarded by most people as a virtue, rather than as the last refuge of a scoundrel as Dr. Johnson would have us believe.

Christianity and Buddhism are both essentially pacifist creeds in theory. But this theoretical pacifism has not prevented their most pious and devout adherents from waging bloody wars among themselves for centuries, whether between Christian England and France, or between Buddhist Burma and Siam, to take only two typical instances. There is no reason to think that Barros was not equally sincere when he was writing the *Decades* as he was when writing *Ropica Pnefma*. In any event, his justification of Portuguese imperialism was quoted approvingly by many later writers, including Frei Serafim de Freitas, O.F.M., in his defence of the Portuguese Crown's claim to the mastery of the Eastern Seas (*De iusto imperio Lusitanorum Asiatico*, Valladolid, 1625), written in refutation of Hugo Grotius' little tract on the freedom of the seas (*Mare Liberum*, 1609).[9]

Reverting to our analysis of *Decade I* : Book 7 does not contain anything of special interest for the modern reader, being devoted largely to the wars between the rajahs of Calicut and Cochin, including the homeric exploits of Duarte Pacheco Pereira, "The Portuguese Achilles". Book 8 is of more interest, being valuable for the chapters dealing with the routes of the spice-trade (ch.1), the Swahili coast of Africa (ch. 4), and the history of the sultanate of the island-city of Kilwa (ch. 6), for which Barros used the Portuguese translation of a local chronicle that has since disappeared.[10]

Book 9 includes three valuable chapters describing successively : "the whole maritime coast of the Orient" from the Red Sea and the Persian Gulf to Japan and the Moluccas: the leading indigenous rulers and kingdoms with which the Portuguese fought and/or traded; and a more detailed description of the petty kingdoms of the Malabar coastal region in

Western India. Finally, Book 10 has a preliminary chapter describing the kingdom of Monomotapa, or the Karinga tribal confederacy of the Muenemutapa in Central Southeast Africa. It contains a fascinating if hearsay account of the now famous ruins of Great Zimbabwe. A modern authority on the history of this region has described this chapter of Barros as being the best and most comprehensive description of the social structure of the Monomotapa written before the late nineteenth century. It is remarkable alike for its compactness, its accuracy, and the critical sense which Barros displays.[11]

(b) *Decade II, 1506-1515*

This Decade, the title of which reads in translation *Second Decade of the Asia of João de Barros, of the deeds which the Portuguese did in the discovery and conquest of the* 1553, *Seas and Lands of the East,* was published on the 24 March nine months after the first, but was meant to be bound and sold together with it, as stated in a footnote at the end of the list of contents in *Decade I.* The period covered is the decisive decade in which the Portuguese established their thalassocracy in the Indian Ocean, beginning with the Viceroy Dom Francisco de Almeida's destruction of a combined Egyptian-Gujarati fleet off Diu (2 Feb. 1509), and completed with the successive conquests of Goa, Malacca, and Hormuz by Afonso de Albuquerque in 1510-15.

Book I does not contain anything of much interest for the modern reader, unless it be the account (in chapter 3) of the island of Socotora, near the mouth of the Red Sea, which the Portuguese occupied from 1507 to 1511. The inhabitants were then "Jacobite Christians of the Abyssinian persuasion,[12] although they do not keep many of their customs; most of the men are called by the names of the Twelve Apostles, and the women Mary. They worship the Cross, and are so devoted to it that they all wear one on the chest. . . . The men are usually well built, of a swarthy colour. The women are fairer and very virile, both in their size, physique, and in their bodily exercise, because they also fight if affronted, just like their husbands. Whence some people maintain that they formerly shunned the company of menfolk, in the same way as the Amazons. Only for the sake of begetting children did they sometimes get men from ships which called at that island. And when the ships did not come, the women cast spells which wafted them thither, in order to get the men. This may be true, both because the women are so virile, as because they are still great spell-binders who do wondrous things".

Book II is largely devoted to Albuquerque's abortive effort to take Hormuz in 1507-08, which gives Barros the opportunity of giving a valuable description and history of this island—then and for over a century the key to the Persian Gulf. For his account of Hormuz, Barros used a Persian chronicler which he had translated for him, as well as Portuguese sources. Professor Jean Aubin has recently had occasion to emphasize the importance of Barros' contribution to the history of the Persian Gulf region and his merits as a historian with a keen awareness of human geography and a genuine interest in the indigenous inhabitants and their past.[13] Book III is mainly concerned with Dom Francisco de Almeida's defeat of the combined Egyptian-Gujarati fleet off Diu (2 February 1509). This has some claim to be considered as one of the decisive battles in the history of the world, since it gave the Portuguese a position of dominance in the Indian Ocean, which they retained for almost exactly a century. This Book ends with an account of Almeida's humiliating death in a futile and ill-conducted skirmish with the Hottentots at Saldanha Bay, near the Cape of Good Hope.

Book IV describes, among other things, the defeat and death of the Marshal, Dom Fernando Coutinho, in an attack on Calicut (chapter one). An incident at Malacca gives Barros an excuse for making an interesting digression concerning the origin and development of the game of chess (chapter 4). In this connection, he refers to a Persian chronicle called "*Tarigh*, which we (had) translated from this language, and which is a summary chronicle of all the kings of Persia until its subjugation by the Muslim Arabs". Book V is devoted to the two conquests of Goa by Afonso de Albuquerque, the first of which proved abortive and the second final. It begins with two chapters describing the historical background of that city and island, and of the neighbouring kingdoms of the Deccan. Barros includes the translation of an old temple-grant, engraved on copper, which had been presented by a Hindu tax-farmer in 1532.[14] He mentions that he had consulted several Hindu and Muslim chronicles, "all of which we secured and which were interpreted for us" (*porque todas estas Chronicas houvemos, e nos foram interpretadas*).

Book VI opens with a valuable chapter on the early history of Malacca and Singapore, for which Barros likewise used oral Malay sources, among others.[15] This is followed by a detailed narrative of the storming and capture of the former city by Afonso de Albuquerque (August, 1511), after a preliminary assault had been beaten back by the defenders. Book VII describes Albuquerque's shipwreck off Sumatra in the flagship *Frol de la Mar* (November, 1511), with the loss of all the priceless treasure pillaged at Malacca, although Albuquerque contrived to save a terrified little slave-girl who clung to him. The same book also deals with Albuquerque's relief of Goa from a siege by the Adil Shah, and his unsuccessful attack on Aden (20 March 1513).

Book VIII recounts *inter alia* Albuquerque's abortive expedition to the Red Sea. The opening chapter has a good description of this region, including a discussion of why the Portuguese called it by this name, "for all the Muslims are astonished that we term it the 'Red Sea'". Incidentally, Barros gives a more objective account of this abortive expedition than do many other writers, beginning with Albuquerque himself who boasted : "at the rumour of our coming, the ships all vanished and even the birds ceased to skim over the water, so overcast was the Red Sea by our arrival and so deserted".[16]

In Book IX the scene shifts mainly to Malaya and Indonesia including a very brief description of the island of Java, and the defeat of the Muslim fleet of Pate Unus, the Sultan of Japara, by Fernão Peres de Andrade (chs. 4-5). This decisive naval victory (January 1513) established the domination of the Portuguese at the eastern end of the Indian Ocean, just as Dom Francisco de Almeida's victory off Diu had done at the western end in 1509.[17] Book X narrates the final conquest of Hormuz by Afonso de Albuquerque. It fittingly and dramatically concludes with the hero's death off Goa on his return voyage, 16 December 1515 : "In disfavour with the king for the sake of men, and in disfavour with men for the sake of the king" (*e assi fico eu mal com El Rey por amor dos homens, e mal com os homens por amor d'El Rey*).

(c) *Decade III, 1516-1525*

This *Decade* is, perhaps, the most interesting one for the modern reader. The naval and military campaigns with which it deals were less momentous than those described in the first two *Decades*, but there is a greater wealth of varied information about Asia. Entitled in translation, *Third Decade of the Asia of João de Barros*: *of the deeds which the Portuguese did in the discovery and conquest of the Seas and Lands of the East*, it was published in 1563 by a different publisher than for the first two, and in a smaller format. The reason for the ten-year delay in publication is not clear, since the text was evidently ready for the press about the same time as the other two.

Book I is mainly devoted to the expedition of Lopo Soares de Albergaria to the Red Sea in 1517, which was even less successful than that of Albuquerqe had been. Although offered the peaceful surrender of Aden by its Muslim governor, he at first declined to accept it, and when he subsequently decided to do so, it was too late. Book II is particularly interesting for Barros' description of early Portuguese relations with Ceylon (chapter 1-3), with Siam (ch. 5), and with China (chapters 7-8).[18] He was exceptionally well-informed about the last two kingdoms. Much of his information on Siam was derived from a Portuguese adventurer "of good family" (*homem de boa linhagem*) named Domingo de Seixas, who had served the king of Siam first as a slave and then as a soldier of fortune for twenty-five years. Barros was the earliest writer to throw light on the doings and habits of the Thai people, as distinct from recording the pomp and ceremony and the wars of their kings, which were supposed by the indigenous chroniclers to constitute history. Barros also anticipated Sir Henry Yule by over three centuries in his tentative identification of Marco Polo's Caugigu with Laos.[19]

As for China, this great empire and its civilisation confessedly fascinated João de Barros. He spared no time, trouble, or expense in learning all that he could about the Middle Flowery Kingdom, which was then in flourishing condition during the heyday of the Ming dynasty. Barros has numerous and invariably favourable references to China and the Chinese throughout his *Decades*. He several times refers to the Chinese books which he had secured, and to an educated Chinese slave whom he had bought to translate them for him, and who was apparently bi-lingual ("he knew how to read and write our language, and was skilled in the use of Arabic numerals").[20] Although this remarkable slave was doubtless his principal informant, Barros also had access to all the correspondence relating to China which came through the India House, including letters which had been smuggled out of Canton jail by Portuguese imprisoned there in 1534-36.[21] Another reliable informant was his friend and colleague, Fernão Peres de Andrade, who led the first and highly successful Portuguese commercial and diplomatic mission to Canton in 1517, and who subsequently became Superintendent of the Royal Dockyard at Lisbon.

The Great Wall of China first appears in a printed European book in this third *Decade*. Marco Polo never mentions it specifically, although he may have had it in mind when writing a passage about Gog and Magog in his famous *Book of the Kingdoms and Marvels of the East*, a Portuguese edition of which was published at Lisbon in 1502.[22] Writes Barros (*Decade III*, Book 2, chapter 7): "This wall is depicted in a geographical map (*carta de Geographia*) of all that land, made by the said Chinese, wherein are likewise shown all the mountains, rivers, cities and towns, with their names written in Chinese characters. We had this brought thence, together with a Chinese who could translate it, as well as some other Chinese books which we likewise secured. And before we got this map, we had also obtained a small volume of cosmography, with maps showing the configuration of the land, and a commentary thereon in the form of an itinerary.[23] And even though this wall was not depicted therein, yet we had been informed about it. And what they originally gave us to understand about this wall, was that it was not entirely continuous, but only built in the passes of some very rugged mountain ranges which ran between the lands of the Chinese and of the Tartars. But now that we have seen how they have depicted it as a continuous whole, we were greatly astonished thereat".

Barros' almost unbounded admiration for China enabled him to take a more tolerant view of the "heathen Chinee" than he or his contemporaries evinced for Muslims and Hindus. Alluding to the common Chinese accusation—which we find repeated in the official *Ming History* or *Ming-shih*—that the Portuguese kidnapped Cantonese children in order to roast and eat them, he comments that this belief is not surprising, since the Portuguese were only newcomers in China, and they themselves believed equally silly stories about strange peoples in distant lands. He stated that the Chinese, conscious of their cultural superiority, "just as the ancient Greeks regarded all other nations as barbarians in comparison with themselves, so the Chinese claim that they have two eyes which enable them to understand everything, whereas we Europeans, since coming into contact with them, have one eye, and all the other nations are blind". The Jesuit missionaries of the eighteenth century found that this comparison was still current in Manchu China.[24] Enumerating Chinese priorities, such as the invention of printing and of artillery, and listing their admirable achievements in the arts and sciences, Barros came to the conclusion that their culture and civilisation were superior to those of the Greeks and Romans—high praise indeed from a humanist scholar of the High Renaissance.

In his analysis of the Chinese judicial system and the provincial administration, Barros notes approvingly : "The officials who administer justice are not allowed to be natives of the districts where they do so, but must be outsiders, in the same way as in this kingdom of Portugal are appointed those magistrates who are called 'outside judges' (*juízes de fóra*). And this is done to ensure that they should administer justice impartially, without being influenced by ties of friendship.[25] On the other hand, the senior military officers have to be natives of the districts in which they are stationed, for they say that local patriotism will make them fight better in defence thereof".

Among the Chinese technical innovations which particularly impressed João de Barros were : the use of carts and wheelbarrows provided with sails to facilitate transportation over level ground; the identification of individuals by means of hand-prints, and the sheathing of junks with a bitumen compounded from slaked-lime and fish-oil, which he terms *lapes*—apparently a word, if not a practice, of Malay origin. He avers that this sheathing was both worm - and water-proof; and he adds that his friend Fernão Peres de Andrade, had introduced it into Portugal, together with the Chinese construction of a stern-gallery (*varandah*) projecting over the rudder.[26] As regards the identification of individuals by their hand-prints, Barros explains that when a married couple were compelled by poverty to sell a child as an indentured servant (*mui-tsai*), and this was done in legal form before the local magistrate : "The father concerned rubs the palm of his right hand in printer's ink and impresses it on the bill of sale, leaving the impress of the whole hand thereon, and then does the same with the impression of the right foot, and the mother does the same ; after which, they receive their money and hand over the child. . . They use this natural method of identification because it is more certain and reliable than any artificial method, and it cannot be duplicated or falsified".[27]

At the end of his description of China in chapter 7 of this book, Barros explains, as he does elsewhere in the *Decades*, that he has a lot more information about this empire, but that he is keeping it for his "Geography", so as not to interrupt the thread of his narrative for too long. This is understandable enough; but it makes the loss of his "Geography" all the more regrettable. The average modern reader would be more interested in reading about the culture and civilisation of the Middle Flowery Kingdom than he would about the "old, unhappy, far-off things and battles long ago" on the fringes of the Indian Ocean, which inevitably take up so much space in the *Decades*, since their author was writing primarily for his own age and not for ours.

Book III is largely devoted to a narrative of events in Malacca and Southeast Asia, including an interesting account of the Mon Kingdom of Pegu (Burma) in chapter 4. Barros repeats here a widespread if palpably ridiculous story that the inhabitants of this kingdom were descended from the sexual union between a dog and a woman, who were the sole survivors of a Chinese junk shipwrecked on that coast. Although somewhat sceptical of this fable, Barros offers the hardly less fanciful alternative explanation that the Peguans were descended from Jews exiled in the time of King Solomon.[28] Chapter 7 has a valuable account of the Maldive Islands, emphasising their staple products of coir and cowries, the latter being exported to Portugal for use in the West-African slave-trade.

Book IV has several chapters devoted to the Christian Coptic kingdom of Ethiopia or Abyssinia, "which we commonly call Prester John". Barros eruditely discusses the origin of this term, and the descent of the ruling dynasty from the son of King Solomon and the Queen of Sheba. He also deals with the first Portuguese embassy to the Negus, of which we have a much fuller account by one of the participants, a secular priest named Francisco Alvares. Barros used this account, but he did not think much of it. He describes it as the work of a man "who wrote a book about this journey on which he went, as also of what he found out there, insofar as his intelligence allowed, more plainly than eruditely written, which has now been translated into Italian".[29] This section of *Decade III* also contains valuable information about the rivalry between the Hindu kingdom of Vijayanagar, or Narsinga as the Portuguese called it, and the Muslim kingdoms of the Deccan, particularly that of Bijapur.

Book V opens with an interesting chapter on the island of Sumatra, and other chapters deal with the relations between the Muslim rulers of this island and the Portuguese of Malacca. Chapter 5 gives a description of the Spice Islands of the Moluccas, and subsequent chapters deal with the celebrated voyage of Fernão de Magalhães and with Portuguese and Spanish rivalry in this remote region. Barros' account is particularly valuable, since he had access not only to all the Portuguese records, but to Spanish documents which had been seized by the Portuguese at Ternate and turned over to him by Duarte de Resende, in acknowledgement of the dedication of *Ropica Pnefma* (p. 47), Naturally enough, Barros made a somewhat selective use of this captured Spanish material; but his account must nevertheless be consulted by all serious students of this epic voyage. Barros was later accused by the Italian cosmographer, Giovanni Battista Gessio, of having deliberately underestimated the width of the South Atlantic Ocean, in order to bring a portion of Brazil within the Portuguese side of the Line of Tordesillas, although Gessio admitted that Barros was more to be trusted than any other Portuguese authority.[30]

Book VI describes *inter alia* the failure of the Portuguese embassy to China headed by Tomé Pires, and the subsequent expulsion of the Portuguese traders from the China coast. This setback was mainly due to the tactless and arrogant behaviour of Simão de Andrade, the unworthy brother of the tactful Fernão Peres. Chapter 4 gives a short description of the Persian Gulf region with emphasis on the island of Bahrein, famous for its dates and its pearl-fishery.

Book VII is mainly devoted to events in Hormuz and the Persian Gulf, with a final chapter on the discovery of the tomb of St. Thomas the Apostle at Meliapor (Mailapur). He was made the patron saint of Portuguese India; but Barros had no use for the "Christians of St. Thomas", whom he stigmatised as being "the most usorious and the most cunning in false weights and measures, and in every manner of buying and selling, in the whole of Malabar, and none of the other Indians can touch them in this".

Book VIII contains an account of the shameful loss of the Portuguese fortress of Pasei in Sumatra to the rising power of Atjeh in May 1524. This disaster was entirely due to the cowardice and incompetence of the garrison commander, who received no punishment for his culpable misconduct.[31] Other chapters deal with the defeat of a Portuguese fleet off the coast of Kwangtung by a Chinese coastguard squadron, and events in Moluccan and in Malayan waters.

Book IX deals with the brief viceroyalty of Dom Vasco da Gama, now Count of Vidigueira (September-December 1524), and with trivial campaigns on the West coast of India. Book X, which is very short, ranges briefly over events from the Red Sea to the Moluccas. There is also mention of an accidental voyage of discovery by a pilot named Gomes de Sequeira to a group of islands which have been variously identified. Some commentators claim that he reached the North coast of Australia; but by far the most convincing identification is Ulithi Atoll, the most spacious atoll in the Western Carolines of Micronesia, as argued by Professor W.A. Lessa with a wealth of anthropological, geographical, linguistic and historical detail ("The Portuguese Discovery of the Isles of Sequeira", in *Micronesia*, Vol. XI, pp. 35-70, Tokyo, 1975).

(d) *Decade IV, 1527-1538*

Published posthumously at Madrid in 1615, this *Fourth Decade of the Asia of João de Barros, of the deeds which the Portuguese did in the discovery and conquest of the Seas and Lands of the East*, was edited by the Cosmographer- and Chronicler-Royal, João Baptista Lavanha, a scholar who received many favours from the Crown despite the fact that he was of Jewish descent on both side (*des todos os quatro costados*).[32]

Lavanha explains in his prologue that he had edited this work by royal command, and that the manuscript version which he had received had passed through several hands since the death of João de Barros. The original material entrusted to him comprised "ten notebooks (*cadernos*) for the ten Books of this *Decade*, torn, incomplete, written in bits and pieces by various hands, and so imperfect that it was obvious this was only the first rough draft. Some leaves were missing, others were left blank, many passages contained repetitions, others were misplaced; some matters unconnected with this history were treated at great length, while some important items were briefly sketched, and others omitted altogether".

He states that he had revised and rewritten the entire text, "imitating, insofar as I could, the style of João de Barros"; and adding, with the approval of a senior minister of the Crown, entire chapters in some places and extensive passages in others, "all of which are indicated by inverted commas".[33]

These interpolations from published sources included copious extracts from Fernão Lopes de Castanheda's rival *History* of 1551-61, Diogo do Couto's *Decade IV*, which had been written in continuation of Barros' first three *Decades*, and Francisco de Andrade's *Chronicle of King John III* (Lisboa, 1613). Lavanha also supplied three maps (of Java, Gujerat, and Bengal) to illustrate the text, although he does not state from where he got them. He stressed that he had made no alterations whatever to an "Apology" which Barros had drafted by way of a prologue to this *Decade*, and which he had found among the other papers, "complete and entirely in his own handwriting", which was not the case with the ten notebooks (*a qual achei entre outros papeis inteira, e escrita de sua mão, que o não eram os dez quadernos*).

Lavanha's editorial work has come in for some severe criticism, most of which, I feel, is misplaced and undeserved. R.S. Whiteway, for instance, alleged : "The fourth *Decade*, which purports to have been made up from notes, was published in 1615; its value is small".[34] This is grossly unfair. Lavanha's version of *Decade IV* did not merely "purport" to have been made up from original notes, but it was in fact based on them. The copious marginal notes and cross-references supplied by Lavanha from other sources are usually helpful and illuminating. They certainly save much trouble for any serious reader who wishes to check statements in the text. Admittedly, it is not always possible to tell where Lavanha has rearranged or re-written the text; but I think it safe to assert that between one-half and two-thirds of it can be ascribed to João de Barros. The three maps may not be of much use to the twentieth century reader, but they were certainly helpful to Lavanha's contemporaries, especially since Iberian histories and chronicles were rarely provided with maps, whether good, bad, or indifferent.[35] On the whole, I feel that Severim de Faria made a fairer judgement than Whiteway when he stated that Lavanha's conscientious editorial work "had made this fourth *Decade* one of the best books which we now have in the vernacular".[36]

Book I deals mainly with events in the Indian Ocean, in Malayan waters, and in the Moluccas. Chapter 12 has a description of Java, which Barros somewhat tentatively split into two separate islands, although he added : "The said Javanese do not make two distinct islands out of Java, but maintain that it is only one". There is also a short account of the pepper-trade in the Sunda region of West Java and East Sumatra, which complemented and competed with that of Malabar in S.W. India.

Book II narrates, *inter alia*, the violent dispute between Lopo Vaz de Sampaio and Pero de Mascarenhas over the succession to the governor-generalship of Portuguese Asia in 1526. This acrimonious quarrel was resolved in favour of the former in India, but he was subsequently deported to Portugal by his successor, and rigorously imprisoned for a couple of years. Several chapters are devoted to Portuguese misrule and atrocities in the Moluccas, which are mainly taken from the works of Fernão Lopes de Castanheda and Diogo do Couto. These misdeeds culminated in the governorship of Dom Jorge de Menezes, a courageous soldier but a sadistic monster. He crowned his cruelties by seizing a village headman and throwing him, with his hands tied behind him, to be worried to death by two fierce mastiffs. When the wretched man waded into the sea for refuge the mastiffs followed, tearing at his flesh, until he turned on them in desperation, seizing one of the animals by the ear with his teeth and dragging it under the water, where both man and beast were drowned, to the horrified amazement of a crowd of onlookers, "who wept to see so brave a man die so cruel a death".

Book III is mainly devoted to the highly controversial governorship-general of Nuno do Cunha (1529-38). The events narrated include his sack of Mombasa, his dubious conduct at Hormuz, and an abortive Portuguese effort to occupy the island of Bahrein in 1529. In chapter 13, Barros mentions an abandoned and ruined city near Basra, which was described to him by his Turkish slave, a native of Cairo (*hum Turco, natural de Cairo*), "a prudent man, and one endowed with a great intelligence and a good memory", who had been there as a soldier. This Turk swore that the ruined city was twice the size of Cairo and the stone houses were still in good condition, although it was only inhabited by one old Muslim caretaker of the Mosque with his family.[37]

Book V opens with a description of the kingdom of Gujarat, and is largely devoted to the doings of the flamboyant Sultan Bahadur who ruled 1526-37,

> *whose daily food is asp, basilisk, and toad,*
> *which makes him have so strong a breath*
> *each night he stinks a queen to death,*

if Samuel Butler's *Hudibras* (1663) may be believed.

Book VI relates the negotiations between Sultan Bahadur and Nuno de Cunha for the establishment of a Portuguese castle at Diu, to which the Sultan eventually and reluctantly agreed in September 1535. This Book also contains an account of the extraordinary voyage of Diogo Botelho from India to Portugal in a cockleshell of a boat, and the inadequate reward which he received for this astounding feat. It is taken mainly from Castanheda's *History*, Book VIII, chapter 203. Other chapters narrate the further misdeeds of the Portuguese in the Moluccas until the arrival of António Galvão, a man of an entirely different stamp from his rascally predecessors.

Book VII continues with the governorship of Nuno da Cunha and the relations of the Portuguese with the neighbouring Indian kingdoms of the Deccan. Book VIII deals mainly with the death of Sultan Bahadur in a shipboard scuffle with the Portuguese in January 1537, and the consequences which flowed from it. In Book IX the scene shifts eastwards to the region of the Bay of Bengal (chapters 1-11), to events in Malayan waters, and to António Galvão's house-cleaning in the Moluccas. This material is again taken mainly from Fernão Lopes de Castanheda.

Book IX describes the first great siege of Diu (September-November 1538) by the Turks and the Gujaratis; its epic defence by António da Silveira; and the sudden retreat of the besiegers when the few surviving defenders were at their last gasp. It also deals with the end of Nuno da Cunha's governorship and his death on the homeward voyage. The heroic part played by some Portuguese women in the defence of Diu is supplied from Lopo de Sousa Coutinho's *Livro Primeiro do cerco que os Turcos puzeram à fortaleza de Diu* (Coimbra,

1556). Special prominence is given to the young and beautiful matron, Dona Isabel da Veiga, one of whose grand-daughters, incidentally, married a grandson of João de Barros.

As mentioned previously, Barros repeatedly states in these *Decades* that he is dealing at greater length with many aspects of Asian history, economy, civilisation and culture, in his forthcoming "Geography" and "Commerce". Neither of these two projected works were quite finished at his death, although the former at least seems to have been relatively far advanced. This problem is discussed on pp. 130-35 below; but it is mentioned here to show that much information which the modern reader may vainly seek in the *Decades* was not overlooked or forgotten by their industrious author, but was reserved for publication elsewhere. Barros' own conception of History, and his reactions to criticism of his monumental work, are clearly evinced in the successive prologues which he wrote for these *Decades*, and which display an increasingly defensive and (at times) bitter tone.

João de Barros was first and foremost an official chronicler, patronised by the Crown. His purpose was essentially an edifying, moral and didactic one, as he makes perfectly clear in each of his prologues. For instance, in the prologue to *Decade III* he writes : "As History is a tilth and field wherein is sown every divine, moral, rational and instrumental doctrine, whoever pastures on its fruit will find it changed into strength of intelligence and memory, thus enabling him to lead a just and perfect life, pleasing alike to God and to men. . . . we inculcate the reading of History for all sorts and conditions of men, as being cheap in price, easy to learn, useful in practice, in war, in joy, in sorrow, in plenty and in want : for it is like a Lesbian rule, which can be applied to anything that we wish to measure with it. . . . But writings which do not have this utility of instruction, besides wasting time which is the most precious thing in life, barbarize the mind and fill the brain with dross from the torrent of words and facts which they convey".

All commentators on the *Decades* of João de Barros agree

that they reflect the official viewpoint of Portuguese expansion in Africa and Asia, which to a large extent coincided with the more general viewpoint, certainly among the educated classes, that this expansion was a patriotic crusade, with Portugal as the standard-bearer of the Faith (*Alferes da Fé*). But if Barros was preaching in this respect to the already converted, he did not escape criticism on other grounds, both then and later. The three chief accusations against him were and are : firstly, that he concentrated on praiseworthy deeds (or what he held to be such), omitting or soft-pedalling those which were to be condemned; secondly, that he was partial in distributing praise and blame to individuals; thirdly, that he sometimes described trivial matters at excessive length, while making only passing mention of much more important events or affairs. There was and is some substance in all these criticisms, but there is also a good deal to be said in his defence.

As regards the first charge, it is true that he sometimes deliberately omitted, or slurred over, actions which were discreditable to his compatriots; but, as the late Ian Macgregor has pointed out, he was reasonably open about it.[38] He explained why he did not wish to emphasize human frailties and vices in the prologue to *Decade III*; one reason being that such a narrative might serve as an incentive rather than as a deterrent to potentially ill-disposed persons. In *Decade II*, when touching on the violent controversy between Afonso de Albuquerque and Dom Francisco de Almeida, he writes : "And forasmuch as our intention in the whole of this our *Asia* is to describe only the war which the Portuguese waged against the infidels, and not that which they had among themselves, let no reader expect to find anything more than what is absolutely necessary to our narrative concerning these disputes between the Viceroy and Afonso de Albuquerque. And the same applies to other similar things which happened later; for we do not wish to stain the story of such illustrious deeds with hatred, envy, malice, greed and other vices which might cause both victors and vanquished to lose a great part of their respective merits".[39]

Despite this frank avowal and despite the inevitable reticences which we find in this as in all official histories to a greater or a lesser degree, Barros is not, in fact, so uncritical or so bland as is implied in the above passages and in others of a like nature which could be quoted. He quite often does give details of crimes, follies and blunders committed by the Portuguese, even if he likewise employs the time-honoured techniques of *suggestio falsi* and *suppresio verbi* on occasion. It must be admitted that his declared objective was not "the truth, the whole truth, and nothing but the truth", but rather as much of the truth as it was good and expedient for his readers to know—an early example of "all the news that is fit to print". It is, perhaps. needless to add that he was not the first nor the last official historian to take this line.

As regards the second charge, the allegation of partiality, this is difficult to sustain or to disprove, as Ian Macgregor has rightly observed. Barros had access to all official correspondence from the East, as well as to much private correspondence therefrom, and a great deal of both was blatantly contradictory. The age-old Portuguese fault of *murmuração* (back-biting, malicious gossip) is very evident in the surviving records; and this trait must have been even more omnipresent in the voluminous records to which Barros had access. He was, of course, fully aware of this national failing, observing of Albuquerque's carping critics at Goa : "a Portuguese is more upset by praise of his neighbours than by neglect of his own merit" (*porque ao Portuguez mais lhe doe o louvor do vizinho, que o esquecimento do seu*).[40] With the best will in the world, it must have been often very hard for João de Barros, as it was for the Crown and its advisers, to distinguish between truth and falsehood in the often conflicting reports, allegations and insinuations which they received from "Golden Goa". If, therefore, he sometimes gave praise where blame was due, and *vice versa*, this maldistribution may have been the fault of the prejudiced and misleading material on which he was compelled to rely rather than of his own personal prejudices.[41]

As regards the third charge, this has much substance in it from a twentieth-century viewpoint, but less from that of his own day and generation. A cultivated and intelligent Florentine, Filippo Sassetti, writing from Portuguese India in 1585, acknowledged that Barros too often made mention of individuals who had participated in unimportant skirmishes; but he added that these individuals, or their descendants, would have been mortally offended if their names had been omitted, and that anyone writing for Portuguese readers would have to record such trivialities. In any event, Barros' primary purpose was to write the history of Portuguese naval and military exploits in the East, and not to provide material for twentieth century social historians and anthropologists.

Barros was well aware that he could not please all his readers. He jocularly observed in the prologue to *Decade II* that when he was interviewing returned expatriates to collect material for his *Asia*, sailors only wanted him to record voyages, shipwrecks, and maritime affairs; knights were only concerned that he should record their martial exploits; geographers were only interested in the configuration of the land; merchants in the price and weight of commodities; the inquisitive reader (*o curioso*) in the exotic manners and customs of strange peoples. Although Barros assured them that they would find his *Asia* to be like a drugstore, where there would be something to satisfy each of them, they were still dissatisfied, since each individual wanted the most space to be devoted to his own sphere of interest. He added that he himself had tried to follow Apollo's dictum of not devoting too much space to any one aspect. If this did not satisfy all his readers, then at least it gave his critics the opportunity to criticise, "which is the sweetest fruit on earth"; so in this way he hoped to please everyone, giving some readers the opportunity "to praise what they like. and others the chance to criticize what they dislike".

As noted previously, Barros was at pains to stress that matters pertaining to social, economic, and maritime history would be discussed at greater length in his projected "Geography", "Navigation" and "Commerce". Unfortunately, he did not live to complete these works, but he can hardly be blamed for that. He did contrive to record a great deal of information about political, economic, and social conditions in his *Decades*, as can be seen from the admirable work of Donald F. Lach, *Asia in the Making of Europe*. In each Book of his *Decades*, Barros is always careful to set the geographical scene and to sketch in the historical background before he tells his story.

He usually made a very good job of it; and the modern historian who is interested in sixteenth-century Asia will ignore Barros at his (or her) peril.[42]

Although Barros did not know any Asian language, he can be termed a pioneer Orientalist. He systematically collected Asian historical and geographical books and manuscripts, and he bought educated slaves to translate them for him. In this way, he was able to utilise an Arabic chronicle of Kilwa in East Africa (*Decade I*, Book 8, ch. VI); a Persian chronicle of Hormuz (*Decade II*, Book 2, ch. II); a Persian dynastic chronicle (*Decade II*, Book 5, ch. II and Book 10, ch. 5); a Persian biography of the Mongol conqueror, Tamerlane (*Decade II*, Book 4, ch. IV); two Arabic and three Persian geographical works with descriptions of the Persian Gulf region *Decade III*, Book 6, ch. IV); a Persian chronicle of the origin of the Moguls (*Decade IV*, Book 6, ch. 1); several chronicles of the kings of Gujarat (*Decade IV*, Book 5, ch. II); another similar one of the rulers of the Deccan (*Decade II*, Book 5, ch. II); a Hindu chronicle of Vijayanagar (*Decade II*, Book 5, ch. II); and a statistical description of the same kingdom (*Decade III*, Book 4, ch. IV); palm-leaf manuscript works (*olas*) on the history, customs, and religions of the peoples of Malabar (*Decade I*, Book 9, ch. 3); and as mentioned previously, several Chinese geographical compendia and atlases (*Decade I*, Book 9, ch. 1 and *Decade III*, Book 2, ch 7). This systematic and discriminating use of primary Oriental sources was something quite unprecedented, and it reflects the greatest credit on João de Barros.

Inevitably, Barros' use of his Asian sources was not impeccable, but his errors in this respect are relatively trivial. As a true Humanist and grammarian he had a fondness for investigating the meanings and origins of words which sometimes led him astray. Some of his explanations of Asian place-names and personal names are consequently wide of the mark; but in the field of etymology it is not only fools who rush in where angels may fear to tread. Thus even the scholarly Donald Ferguson, who chides Barros for his Sinhalese "etymological atrocities", fell into a similar trap himself; for his otherwise model monograph, *Letters from*

Portuguese captives in Canton, 1534-36, is marred by equally ludicrous mis-identifications of Chinese terms. Similarly, R.S. Whiteway's criticism of Barros in his *Rise of the Portuguese Power in India* has been rebutted by the late Ian Macgregor, who pointed out that Whiteway's account of the Portuguese in Malacca was less correct than that of Barros.[43]

A more serious allegation made by Whiteway, and one repeated by many later writers, was that Barros, as an authority on India, ranks below those who knew the country. To some extent this is undeniably true, although it is certainly not so in every instance. Barros was sometimes right when Gaspar Correa (*c.* 1496-*c.* 1567), Fernão Lopes de Castanheda (149?-1559), and Diogo do Couto (*c.* 1542-1616) were wrong, although these three all spent many years in India.

Barros was twitted with his lack of personal experience of Asia by Fernão Lopes de Castanheda, who had gone out to Goa with his father in 1528 and stayed in the East for about ten years. He observed in the prologue to Book I of his *History* (1551) : "And thus I visited the places in which were done the deeds that I would have to describe, in order that I could write more accurately about them; for many writers have made great mistakes in what they wrote, because they had never seen the places about which they write". Reverting to this theme in Book III of his *History* (1552), Castanheda reiterated : "It was a great advantage to me that I was not merely satisfied with what people told me, but that I spent some time in India and I saw things there with my own eyes. For if this had not been so, I could easily have been misled by the reports of others, as one who had never set eyes on that region, nor could tell whether or not things could be done in the places where they were alleged to have happened".

Castanheda also boasted in the same Prologue : "And I certify this to Your Highness, that I did not learn it in my house; nor did I send to ask about it in writing from those who knew it, . . . or through my employment, or through any other cause, but I went to learn it in India, experiencing in the voyage wild and terrible storms, during which I saw myself on the point of death and without hope of life, suffering great hunger and severe thirst; and there I went through a thousand dangers in frightful battles with countless cannon and musket balls . . . . And it was among them that I learned the truth of what I had to write . . . . And for that reason, those who have to write histories must make the efforts that I did, and see the lands of which they intend to treat, as I did, because the genius that knows how to describe something which it has never seen, must be a very supernatural one. This accusation cannot be levelled at me, for I saw storms, I saw battles by land and sea, ships shattered and walls battered and enemies vanquished, and I speak from actual experience".[44]

Although Castanheda does not mention João de Barros by name, it is perfectly clear that these criticisms are directed primarily if not entirely at him. Both had been working on their respective histories for many years, Barros since 1520 and Castanheda since 1528. Both had freely and frequently interviewed men who had returned from the East, as they both were at pains to point out. Castanheda was a beadle and a librarian at Coimbra University in 1552, when Barros was Factor of the India House at Lisbon; Portugal was a small country with a small educated population; and it is virtually certain that they must have been aware by 1550—and probably long before—that they were both engaged on a similar project and that both their works were nearing completion. Both of them emphatically claimed priority, and Castanheda alleged in his third Book that certain highly placed people at Court were trying to impede the publication of his work.

Barros, on his side, without actually naming Castanheda, clearly had the latter chiefly in mind when he penned his violent denunciation of unqualified writers who filled their chronicles with useless details and who could not distinguish between the important and the trivial. It is quite possible, indeed probable, that it was Barros who was mainly responsible for blocking the publication of Books Nine and Ten of Castanheda's *History* after 1561. This is the more likely, since in 1563 he urged that the chronicles of which he so strongly disapproved should be sold by order of the Crown to shopkeepers for use as wrapping-paper.[45]

Fernão Lopes de Castanheda and João de Barros were mutually unjust to each other. Their relative priority in print was only a difference of a few months, and of no practical significance to posterity. Barros' *Decades* were better planned and better arranged than Castanheda's *History*, and Barros had a global viewpoint and an appreciation of geography which were lacking in Castanheda. But the latter was less inhibited than Barros, and his prose was less majestic and more spontaneous. Castanheda devotes even more space to the minutiae of skirmishes by land and sea than does Barros, and he did not sketch in the historical and geographical background so clearly and firmly. But the *Decades* and the *History* are both highly creditable to their respective authors. The modern reader can afford to regard them as complementary rather than as rival works.[46]

We have seen that Barros and Castanheda both stressed the trouble which they took to interview Portuguese who had returned from Asia. Barros had the advantage here, by virtue of his key position at the heart and centre of the colonial administration; but Castanheda tells us that he travelled at his own expense all over Portugal interviewing returned fidalgos, apart from those whom he had met while in Asia. Among Barros' informants was the famous traveller and adventurer, Fernão Mendes Pinto, who was his chief authority about Japan, until the Jesuits persuaded him that he would do better to consult their missionary reports from the Land of the Rising Sun. Barros, therefore, had a preview of the famous *Peregrination*, since the first draft of this unique masterpiece was ready by 1569.[47]

Barros deliberately cultivated a stately prose style in the *Decades*, since he was consciously trying to erect a monumental literary work. He therefore tried to make his writing as majestic and measured as he could. His moral and didactic stances sometimes led him into sententiousness and pomposity, but, on the whole, less than one might expect. Like his Latin model, he sometimes puts edifying speeches into the mouths of his protagonists, although some of them may well have a basis of fact. For instance, the speech which he puts into the mouth of Caramansa, the Negro ruler who tried to dissuade Diogo de Azambuja from building the fortress of St. George of the Mine in Guinea, rings singularly true. It almost certainly reflects the doubts and fears which the former felt.[48] Barros also enlivens his narrative with occasional flashes of humour, as well as with caustic asides and topical allusions. He can coin a telling phrase. *The praia de lágrimas*, "beach of tears", was first applied by him to the strand of Restelo, where the weeping onlookers saw the departure of Vasco da Gama's pioneer armada, and whence so many men embarked in the annual India fleets, never to return.[49]

Barros undoubtedly enriched the vocabulary of his compatriots with some of the Asian terms which he helped to fix in the language by embedding them in the prose of his *Decades*. As a foreigner, I would not like to expatiate at length on the merits of Barros as a prose stylist; but I think that most people who have read the *Decades* in the original would agree that his style is usually clear, careful, and stately, which is what he wished it to be.[50]

Whatever his merits as a stylist—and possibly as a major influence on Camões when the "prince of Portuguese poets" was composing the *Lusíadas*—it remains true that Barros was read, is read, and will continue to be read, more for the historical interest and importance of his *Decades* than for anything else which he wrote. Over a century ago, John Crawfurd, a scholar well acquainted with Southeast Asia, observed of João de Barros : "He had the best means of obtaining accurate information; and, for the time in which he lived, certainly made a faithful and judicious use of his opportunities".[51] That verdict still stands. Recent historical research has only served to enhance the reputation of João de Barros in this as in other respects.

NOTES

1. Hernâni Cidade, *Portugal Histórico-Cultural* (2nd ed. Lisboa, 1968), p. 141 ("Isso nos impoe atentar no estilista e no gramático, porque

ele é, na evolução da língua portuguesa, da mesma importância que na evolução da historiografia nacional)".

2. Barros has slipped slightly here, as the name first given to Cabral's new-found land (if such it was) was *Vera Cruz*, "True Cross".
3. *Década I*, Livro 9, cap. i : "O debuxo da qual pedra o anno passado de mil e quinhentos quarenta e oito me mandaram em tres papees". Here and elsewhere my references to and quotes from the *Décadas* are taken from the first editions; but as most of my readers will only have access to later editions, I have omitted the page references.
4. Donald F. Lach, *Asia in the making of Europe*, I, *The Century of Discovery* (Chicago University Press, 1965), Book I, p. 190.
5. The Hakluyt Society edition by C.R. Beazley and Edgar Prestage, *The Chronicle of the Discovery and Conquest of Guinea* (2 vols. London, 1896-99), is now out of date and is superseded by later research. Pending the publication of Professor Peter Russell's forthcoming work on the Portuguese voyages of discovery in the 15th century, Zurara may most conveniently be consulted in Léon Bourdon *et al* (eds.), *Gomes Eanes de Zurara. Chronique de Guinée*, (Ifan-Dakar, 1960).
6. Barros also used the work of another predecessor and contemporary, the royal chronicler Rui de Pina (*c.* 1440-1522) for his accounts of Portuguese relations with various West African kingdoms. Cf. J.W. Blake, *Europeans in West Africa, 1450-1560* (Hakluyt Society, 2 vols., London, 1942), pp. 4-18, 78-86.
7. W.B. Greenlee (*ed.* and *trans.*), "*The Voyage of Pedro Alvares Cabral to Brazil and India from contemporary documents and narratives* (Hakluyt Society, London, 1938).
8. The references is to a series of papal bulls, briefs, and donations, of which the most important are analysed in C.R. Boxer, *The Portuguese Seaborne Empire, 1415-1825* (London & New York, 1969), pp. 20-23.
9. *Fr. Serafim de Freitas, O.F.M , Do justo Império Asiatico dos Portugueses* (eds. Marcello Caetano and Miguel Pinto de Meneses, Lisboa, 1960).
10. James S. Kirkman, *Men and Monuments on the East African Coast* (London, 1964), pp. 192-202.
11. W G.L. Randles, *L'Image du Sud-Est Africain dans la littérature Européene au XVIe siècle* (Lisboa, 1959), pp. 53-77, especially p. 71. The same work contains an annotated French translation of this chapter, pp. 183-96. Cf. also the same author's "Matériaux pour the histoire du Sud-Est African jusqu'au XVIIIe siècle" in *Annales. Economies. Societiës. Civilisations* (Sept.-Oct. 1963), pp. 956-80; Peter Garlake, *Great Zimbabwe* (London, 1973), pp. 51-62, 69, 174, 176, 200.
12. "Todos são Christãos Jacobitas da casta dos Abexijs". They were so called from Jacob Baradoeus, Bishop of Edessa in the 6th century,

who taught that Jesus Christ had but one nature and that the Divine. Also known as the Monophysite Syrian Christians who were in communion with the Monophysite Copts of Egypt, owing allegiance to the Patriarch of Antioch. Cf. Jozé Pereira da Costa, *Societera e o dominio Português no Oriente*, reprint from the Revista da Universidade de Coimbra, XXIII, 323-71 (1973).

13. Barros repeatedly refers to this Persian general chronicle, *Tarigh* (*Ta'rikh*, or *Tawarikh*, "History"), but he also used another one limited to the kings of Hormuz, the *Shahnama*. Cf. G. Schurhammer, S.J., *Franz Xaver. Sein Leben und seine Zeit, II* (*2*), *Indien und Indonesien, 1547-1549* (Freiburg, 1971), pp. 498-99, Jean Aubin, "Le Royaume d'Ormus" in *Mare Luso-Indicum*, II (Geneva 1973), pp. 77-187.

14. Lacu (or Locu) Naik, a wealthy and erudite Brahmin of Goa, who was subsequently converted to Christianity in 1548. Barros realised that the translation he obtained was deficient in some ways, but he drew from it the erroneous conclusion that Christianity existed in Goa in Pre-Muslim times. See the commentary by Panduronga Pissurlencar, *Goa Pré-Portuguesa através dos Escritores Lusitanos dos séculos XVIe XVII* (Bastorá-Goa, 1962), pp. 18-23, and the sources there quoted. The original comprised three (not one) copperplates with an inscription in Sanskrit and some lines in Kanarese, dating from 1391.

15. "E segundo os póvos Malaios dizem (de quem nós recebemos esta relação)". For the interest and importance of Barros' account of pre-Portuguese Malacca and Malaya, see the discussion in Donald F. Lach, *Asia in the making of Europe*, I (2), pp. 505-12. Cf. also M.A.P. Meilink-Roclofsz, *Asian Trade and European influence in the Indonesian Archipelago, 1500-1630* (The Hague, 1962), pp. 36-59.

16. Carlo M. Cipolla, *Guns and Sails in the early period of European expansion, 1400-1700* (London, 1965), p. 137, quotes this passage in a slightly abridged form from one of Albuquerque's dispatches in 1513, and adds : "This was not rhetorical prose". With respect, rhetorical prose is exactly what it was, as is clear from Barros' less euphoric account and from R.S. Whiteway, *The Rise of the Por tuguese Power in India, 1497-1550* (Westminster, 1899), pp. 155-57, and M.A.P. Meilink-Roclofsz. *Asian Trade and European Influence, 1500-1630* (1962), p. 116.

17. For Pate Unus see M.A.P. Meilink-Roelofsz, *Asian Trade and European Influence, 1500-1630*, index, *in voce.*

18. For Barros' references to Ceylon, see the annotated translation by Donald Ferguson, "The History of Ceylon from the earliest times to 1600 A.D., as related by João de Barros and Diogo do Couto", in *Journal of the Ceylon Branch of the Royal Asiatic Society*, Vol. XX (Colombo, 1908), pp. 20-58; Donald F. Lach, *Asia in the Making of Europe*, I (1), pp. 342-47.

19. Joaquim de Campos, *Early Portuguese accounts of Thailand* (27-page reprint from the *Journal of the Siam Society*, Vol. 32, Bangkok 1940).
20. *Decade* I, Book 9, ch. 1.
21. Donald Ferguson (ed. and trans.), *Letters from Portuguese captives in Canton, 1534-1536* (Bombay, 1902); G. Schurhammer, S.J., *Die Zeitgenössischen Quellen zur Geschichte Portugiesisch-Asiens, 1538-1552* (Rome, 1962), pp. 17-18, 487.
22. H. Yule and H. Cordier (eds.), *The Book of Ser Marco Polo, the Venetian, concerning the kingdoms and marvels of the East* (3 vols., London, 1903-20), Vol. I, pp. *110*, 292-94.
23. Probably an atlas or geographical compendium of the type of the *Kuang-yü-t'u*, for which see Walter Fuchs, *The 'Mongol Atlas' of China by Chu-Ssu-pen and the Kuang-yü-t'u. With 48 facsimile maps dating from about 1555* (Peking, 1946); C.R. Boxer, *South China in the Sixteenth Century* (ed. Hakluyt Society, London, 1953), index *in voce.*
24. See the letter of André Pereira S.J., d. Peking, 30 May 1737, *apud* C.R. Boxer, "A Note on the interaction of Portuguese and Chinese medicine at Macao and Peking, 16th-18th centuries", 26-page reprint from the *Boletim do Instituto Luís de Camões*, Vol. VIII, Macau, 1974, p. 12.
25. The *Juizes de fora*, or *Juizes de fora parte*, were first appointed in Portugal during the early 14th century, and the system was expandde after the Black Death. See Joel Serrão (ed.), *Dicionário de História de Portugal*, Vol. II (1965), pp. 641-42, and the sources there quoted.
26. "E elle foy o primeiro hómem que por ver este bom uso aos Chijs, lançou lápez ás náos e navios que levou, o que se óra costuma entre nós: e assi as varandas sobre o leme fora do corpo da náo" (*Decade III*, Book 2, ch. viii). Cf. Joseph Needham *et al.*, *Science and Civilisation in China*, Vol. IV, *Physics and Physical Technology*, Part III, *Civil Engineering and Nautics* (Cambridge UP. 1971), pp. 413-14, 648, 698, although no mention is made of João de Barros' priority.
27. *Decade III*, Book 6, ch. ii. cf. Luis de Pina, "Uma prioridade portuguesa do século XVI. João de Barros e a dactiloscopia oriental", in *Arquivo da Repartição de Antropologia Criminal*, IV (Porto, 1936), pp. 20-27. I owe a xerox of this rare article to the kindness of Senhora Graça de Almeida Rodrigues.
28. Donald F. Lach, *Asia in the making of Europe*, I (2), p. 553, for a discussion of this and related sexual practices.
29. Cf. C.F. Beckingham and G.W.B. Huntingford (eds.), *The Prester John of the Indies, being the narrative of the Portuguese Embassy to Ethiopia in 1520, written by Father Francisco Alvares* (2 vols. Hakluyt Society, ed. Cambridge 1961).
30. *Parecer* of Giovanni Battista Gesio (or Gessio), signed and dated Madrid, 24 November 1579, *apud* J.P. Leite Cordeiro, "Documentos Quinhentistas Espanhóis referentes à Capitania de São Vicente"

(in *Revista do Instituto Historico de São Paulo*, Vol. XLVI, pp. 314 ff.). For Gesio see Luís de Albuquerque, *A Projecção da náutica Portuguesa Quinhentista na Europa* (Coimbra, 1972); Armando Cortesão, *Cartografia e Cartógrafos Portugueses dos séculos XV e XVI*, Vol. II (Lisboa, 1935), pp. 278-83. For Barros as an authority on Magellan's voyage see the article by L. Torodash in "Magellan Historiography", *Hispanic-American Historical Review*, Vol. 51 (May 1971), p. 318.

31. André Henriques. Gaspar Correia in his *Lendas da India*, Vol. II, pp. 766-69, 780, 790-96, is even more critical than Barros over the misconduct which led to the fall of this fortress, the first one lost by the Portuguese in Asia.
32. For João Baptista Lavanha (15??-1625) and the singular favours which this remarkable "New Christian" received from the Crown, including the admission of two of his daughters to a convent at Madrid in a ceremony attended by Philip IV, his French Queen and the Countess of Olivares in 1623, see *Ethnos*, XII, pp. 294-361.
33. ". . . accrescentei, com approvação de hum Ministro de Sua Magestade a quem se cometteo, capitulos inteiros e grandes pedaços em outros (que tudo vai notado com comas)". Unfortunately, the editor of the 1777 edition omitted these quotation marks, which may have misled Whiteway and others who have used this untrustworthy edition (now available in a facsimile reprint, Lisbon, 1973). The vicissitudes which befell Barros' original draft until the publication of the composite *Decade IV* in 1615, are narrated at length with copious extracts from archival sources by António Baião in his introduction to the Coimbra 1932 edition of *Década I*, pp. lviii-lxxiii. The "Ministro de Sua Magestade" who authorised Lavanha's editorial work was probably Cristovão Soares, the Secretary of State for Portugal.
34. R.S. Whiteway, *Rise of the Portuguese Power in India*, p. xi.
35. The origins of these maps engraved by James Astor have not yet been traced. See Armando Cortesão & A.C. Teixeira da Mota, *Portugaliae Monumenta Cartographica* (6 vols., Coimbra 1960-63), Vol. IV, p. 71.
36. ". . . de modo que ficou esta *Quarta Decada* hum dos melhores livros que hoje temos em nosso vulgar" (*Discursos Vários*, 1624, fls. 52-53).
37. The reference seems to be to the ruins of Old Basra, founded by the Caliph Omar in 636 A.D., some eight miles (not leagues) S.W. of the modern Basra, later the site of the town of Zoheir (Zubayr). Professor S. Ozbaran kindly informs me that this Turkish slave may possibly be identified with a courier (*cavus*) named Bali, who was captured by the Portuguese, and whose fief (*timar*) was given to his brother Iskandar in 1556, (personal communication).
38. Ian A. Macgregor, "Some aspects of Portuguese historical writing

of the 16th and 17th centuries on South East Asia" (in D.G.E. Hall, ed., *Historians of South East Asia*, London, 1961, pp. 172-199), p. 182 of this very perceptive essay.

39. *Decade II*, Book 3, ch. viii. More light on this vicious rivalry between Almeida and Albuquerque, in which no holds were barred, will be found in Jean Aubin's forthcoming *Mare Luso-Indicum*, Vol. III.
40. *Decade II*, Book 5, ch. xi: "porque ao Portuguez mais lhe doe o louvor do vizinho, que o esquescimento do seu". There is a very similar passage earlier in the same *Decade*, Book 3, ch. ix: "porque aos Portuguezes mais lhes doe, e se indignam polo que dam a seu vizinho, que polo que elles não recebem".
41. This was especially marked during the controversial governorship of Nuno da Cunho (1529-38), for which the archival material was—and to a lesser extent still is—abundant and contradictory. Cf. G. Schurhammer, S.J. "The India Letters of 1533", and "Cartas de Martim Afonso de Sousa, 1534-49", in his *Gesammelte Studien*, II, *Orientalia* (Rome-Lisboa, 1963), pp. 153-207. Barros stated (*Decade IV*, Book 10, ch. xxi) that he had received two trunks or chests (*arcas*) containing the papers of Nuno da Cunha, which enabled him to give a more balanced presentation than would otherwise have been possible.
42. In addition to the frequently quoted work of Donald F. Lach, *Asia in the making af Europe*, and Ian Macgregor's article quoted in note (38) above, critical and on the whole decidedly favourable evaluations of João de Barros as a historian of Asia will be found in C.R. Boxer, *Three Historians of Portuguese Asia*: *Barros, Couto and Bocarro* (Macau, 1948); J.B. Harrison, "Five Portuguese historians: Barros, Couto, Bocarro, Castanheda and Correa", in C.H. Philips (ed.) *Historians of India, Pakistan and Ceylon* (London, 1961); G. Schurhammer, S.J., *Franz Xaver*, II (2) *Indien und Indonesien, 1547-1549* (Freiburg, 1971), pp. 440-41, where however, Lisboa should be substituted for Coimbra as the place of publication of the 1777-78 edition of the *Decadas*.
43. C.R. Boxer, *Three Historians of Portuguese Asia* (1948) p. 11; Ian Macgregor, "Some aspects of Portuguese historical writing on S.E. Asia", p. 182.
44. Fernão Lopes de Castanheda (1555-1559), author of the *Historia do Descobrimento e Conquista da India pelos Portugueses*, Books I-VIII of which were published at Coimbra in 14??-61, twenty-one chapters of the lost Book IX were edited by C. Wessels, S.J. at The Hague in 1929, and a new edition of all the foregoing by Pedro de Azevedo, Coimbra University Press, 4 volumes, 1924-33. Book X has disappeared, and we know from an autograph note by Damião de Góis in the (ex-Salva) copy of the first edition in the library of the Hispanic Society at New York that the Queen-Regent ordered the suppression of Books IX-X. Góis gives no reason for the reversal

of her patronage, and Book III had been dedicated to her. Castanheda served in India, 1529-38, but it is not clear whether he got as far as the Moluccas, as Diogo do Couto tentatively stated on hearsay evidence.

45. For a more detailed discussion of the rivalry between Barros and Castanheda see A.J. Saraiva, *História da Cultura em Portugal*, III (1962), pp. 213-220.
46. I.A. Macgregor, "Some aspects of Portuguese historical writing on S.E. Asia", pp. 191-92, for a brief but perceptive comparison between Barros and Castanheda.
47. Letter of Cipriano Sares, S.J., d. Coimbra, 22 Feb. 1569, to Diego Mírón, S.J. at Rome, *apud* G. Schurhammer, *Gesammelte Studien*, II, *Orientalia* (Lisboa-Roma, 1963), p. 557.
48. *Decade I*, Book 3, ch. ii. Rui de Pina has a very similar account of the foundation of São Jorge da Mina, with a much shorter version of Caramansa's speech. English translation in J.W. Blake, *Europeans in West Africa, 1450-1560*, pp. 70-78, especially pp. 74-75. It seems likely that both Pina and Barros were using the same original reports.
49. *Decade I*, Book 4, ch. ii.
50. For a good evaluation of João de Barros' literary style see Hernini Cidade, *Portugal Histórico-Cultural* (Lisboa) 1968, pp. 136-40, 152-67.
51. John Crawfurd, *A Descriptive Dictionary of the Indian Islands and Adjacent Countries* (London, 1856), p. 40. Among modern Orientalists who have made extensive and judicious use of Barros' *Decades* are Jean Aubin in *Mare Luso-Indicum*, II (Geneva, 1973), pp. 77-179, and Pierre-Yves Manguin, *Les Portugais sur les côtes de Viet-nam et du Campá. Etude sur les routes maritimes et les relations commerciales, d'après des sources portugaises, XVe-XVIIIe siècles* (Paris, 1972).

7

INCOMPLETE, UNPUBLISHED, AND MISSING WORKS

Some of these have already been mentioned in passing, but it will be convenient to group them together here. The most important was undoubtedly the world-geography on which Barros was engaged simultaneously with the *Decades*, and to which he makes frequent and specific allusions. Written in Latin, for the sake of wider circulation among international humanists, and entitled *Geographia Universalis*, the first draft was virtually completed by the time that Barros died, and it was seen by a Spanish Carmelite friar, Mariano Azaro, in October 1583.[1] He stated that it then belonged to a son of João de Barros named Francisco; but the chronicler never had a son of that name. Fr. Azaro probably means the eldest son, Jerónimo, who certainly inherited some of his father's manuscripts. In any event the excited friar gives a brief description of the contents, which seems to be reliable. According to him, it was organised on a regional basis, and the maps were accompanied by explanatory texts, giving not only the situation of each region, but its history, rites, laws and customs, "after the manner of Strabo", as well as fixing the respective latitudes with great precision.[2]

With the much greater material at his command than was available to any of the classical geographers, Barros was naturally able to correct and vastly improve on their work; but Fray Azaro notes that he did so with due respect for them and especially for the work of Ptolomey. From Barros' own references to his "Universal Geography" in the *Decades*, we know that it was divided into four parts, of which the fourth treated particularly of all the islands in the world. This plan, states Severim de Faria, was subsequently followed by Giovanni Botero in his celebrated and very popular *Universal Relations*.[3] From references in the *Decades*, it is also apparent that Barros gave a detailed description of the mariner's astrolabe and other nautical instruments in this lost work.

The Spanish friar also saw at the same time the unfinished draft of João de Barros' manuscript treatise on "Commerce" (p. 98 above). He stated that it comprised forty "Books", and from what he had seen of some of the chapters, he was convinced that it was a truly admirable work. It would, he wrote, make better and more reliable reading than Pliny's *Natural History*, and it would be of inestimable value to merchants and traders. In this unfinished work, Barros described *inter alia* the history of coinage, the varying values of money, the prices of merchandise, freights, and insurance, "since the beginning of the world" (*sic*). No relevant detail, however insignificant, had been omitted, "for João de Barros was the best-informed man who has lived hitherto", and he took immense trouble to sift, collate, and compare the information which he so laboriously procured.[4] Even making due allowance for the worthy Carmelite's excited enthusiasm, we can see that the loss of these two great works was a very serious one, and that João de Barros was a pioneer in economic history.

Fray Mariano Azaro further alleged that he had previously seen the manuscript of *Decade IV*, "which is complete, revised by its author"' and ready for the press. He expected that it would soon be published, but in this he was mistaken.[5] Even if the manuscript was in the finished state which he ascribed to it, by the time it (or else the original rough drafts) reached the hands of João Baptista Lavanha, it required drastic revision and editing, as we have seen (p. 111). On the other hand, Fr. Azaro may have been correct when he asserted that the manuscript which he saw was ready for printing, since Jerónimo de Barros claimed that he had submitted such a revised and corrected draft for censorship and approval by the Inquisition in 1578, and he had received a couple of Crown grants for his real or alleged editorial work. But Jerónimo died in 1586, and it is not clear whether it was portions of this manuscript, or of an earlier and rougher draft, which finally came into the hands of João Baptista

Lavanha, after having passed through those of the royal chronicler, Duarte Nunes de Lião, and various others, including a learned Spanish Jesuit, Pedro Paulo Ferrer.[6]

Of the other unfinished works which complemented the *Decades of Asia*, the projected *Africa* and *Europe* do not seem to have passed the stage of preliminary drafts or notes. In his autograph "*Apology by way of Prologue*" to *Decade IV*, which was evidently written towards the end of his life, Barros implies that owing to the critical reception which his first three Asian *Decades* had encountered from his compatriots, he was absolved from his promise to complete the series by writing "Africa" and "Europe". Jerónimo de Barros, when petitioning the Crown for the publication of his father's draft *Decade IV*, declared that if this work was printed, he would then supply the unfinished work on "Africa", which his father had left, if the Crown required him to do so. Manuel de Faria e Sousa later asserted that this draft was then in the possession of Dom Rodrigo da Cunha, Archbishop of Lisbon in 1635-43, and that he himself had had access to it. If so, this draft, or drafts, subsequently seem to have disappeared.[7] The projected American portion of the *Decades*, provisionally entitled by João de Barros as "The Land of the Holy Cross", does not seem to have gotten very far. At any rate, Severim de Faria, writing in 1624, asserts that no trace of it was ever found.

Of the pedagogical and didactic works in this group, Barros mentions (*Decade II*, Bk. 1, ch. II), a manuscript entitled *Esfera da Estructura das Cousas* ("Sphere of the Structure of Things"), which contained a substantial section wholly devoted to architecture.[8] This work seems to have vanished without trace. Severim de Faria lists it as still unpublished in 1624, but he does not give its provenance and he evidently had not seen it. In the *Diálogo de Viciosa Vergonha*, Barros mentions having written a treatise on moral causes or problems (*Tratado de Causas ou Problemas Moraes*). Severim de Faria claimed that the original manuscript was still extant in 1624, being then in the possession of a nephew of João de Barros, who was living at Viseu, as he had been assured by several reliable informants.[9] Although this work has not yet come to light, one may reasonably hope that there is a chance it may do so.

In 1561, Barros composed a long didactic poem entitled *Exelamação contra os Vicios* ("Denunciation of Vices"), which was dedicated to his friend, João Rodrigues de Sá de Meneses. It consisted of more than 460 *redondilhas,* strophes of eight syllables, and is sometimes referred to as the *Abusões do Tempo* ("Abuses of Time"), which is the title Barros himself gave it in the Apology-Prologue to his *Decade IV.* Severim de Faria assures us that it had been seen and read by an acquaintance of his, the *Licenciado* Francisco Galvão de Mendanha, who told him that it was divided into three parts and that the first verse began with the lines *Em aquella eternamente Alta luz inacessível.* It originated as a defence of Barros' own literary predilections and occupations, since friends and relations had accused him of wasting his time in writing historical, moral, and didactic works. He retorted in this poem by justifying their usefulness, and by describing those works (including perhaps, Lopes de Castanheda's *History*) which really were to be condemned[10] :

Diogo Barbosa Machado in his monumental bibliography lists the following three works of João de Barros as being still unpublished when he wrote in 1747 :

1. "Natural History of the East, describing the plants and animals of those regions, and the artificial works pertaining to the commutation and commerce of both these materials." "This work is mentioned in *Decade I,* Book 6, chapter 4." Reference to the place cited, shows that this is merely a small section of his vast unfinished work on "Commerce", dealing with the betel-nut and its uses.
2. "Summary description of all the regions of the world, especially of the Indies both those of Castile and of Portugal, it also treats at length of the art of navigation, together with the sphere in Portuguese, together with the rules of the Sun, the North, and

other courses and latitudes, together with many other things needful for Navigators". Barbosa Machado adds that it was then preserved in the library of the Marquis of Abrantes and seemed to be the original. It began : "You should know that at the circles of the horizons, etc."
This sounds suspiciously like a Portuguese version of some portion(s) of the Latin "Geographia Universalis".

3. "History of the Kings of Persia, Great Tamerlane, and Prester John. Left incomplete and preserved in the Royal Library". Presumably these works perished in the earthquake and fire of 1 November 1755, which destroyed the royal library. They were translations made for Barros from the indigenous chronicles concerned. In *Decade II*, Book 4, ch. IV. Barros mentions that a great part of the Tamerlane chronicle had already been translated for him.

Last not least, João de Barros was the author of a Latin grammar, of which the only surviving manuscript copy is not quite complete and was lost for many years. Recovered some fifty years ago, it is now available in print, thanks to the scholarship of Senhora Maria Leonor Buescu and to the munificence of the Calouste Gulbenkian Foundation.[11] Entitled *Grammatices Rudimenta*, it was dedicated to the Infanta Dona Maria, daughter of King John III, with whom Barros was clearly on almost paternal terms (p. 92). This beautifully illustrated manuscript in the National Library at Lisbon, although not in the hand of Barros, is evidently the original dedication copy. The last chapter is missing and the manuscript is undated; but Senhora Buescu has adduced good reasons for considering it to have been compiled about the year 1540. Intended to help the young princess to learn Latin, it is organised on an inductive method with schematic figures (a tree, a hand, etc.) which help to ease the child's lessons by likening them to a game.

When to the impressive list of the works of João de Barros published between 1522 and 1615 we add these which are listed in this chapter, it is clear beyond a peradventure that not only was his the pen of a ready writer, but that we are dealing with one of the outstanding humanists of the sixteenth century.

NOTES

1. "... no de todo punto limada, sino asi de primera deboço", Letter of Fr. Mariano Azaro, barefoot Carmelite friar, to an unidentified minister of the Crown, d. Lisboa, 9 October 1583 (British Museum, Additional Mss. 28451, fls. 360-63). I have a xerox copy.
2. "... con sus tablas muy puntuales de cada region, y sus historias a modo de Estrabon, de los ritos, leyes, costumbres, y grande precision en las alturas". Strabo (*c.* 63 B.C.-*c* 21 A.D.), whose Geography of the Roman Empire in 17 Books stressed human geography, included accounts of the politics and history of the various peoples he described.
3. João de Barros, *Decade I*, Book 2, ch, i and Book 4, ch. ii; *Decade II*, Book 8, ch. ii. Severim de Faria, *Discursos* (1624), fls. 47-48. Giovanni Botero (1533-1617), author of a series of very popular descriptive geographical works. His *Le relationi universali*, first published at Rome in 1591, was translated into English by Robert Johnson and published at London in 1601, under the title of *The Travellers breviat, or an historical description of the most famous kingdoms in the world*, and reprinted six times before 1640.
4. "... porque Juan de Varros fue el hombre mas bien informado que hasta oy a avido, porque de una sola cosa no se contentava com menos relaçiones por acotejar la verdad y en esto gasto su edad y todo el favor que destos reyes de Portugal tubo sin pensar a otro interes".
5. "La 4ª decada del Asia y escrevi a V.S. Illustríssima que esta entera y revista del mesmo autor. Creo que presto saldra à luz, que es letura muy digna de ser leyda".
6. António Baião, *Documentos inéditos* (1917), pp. 108-114; Ibidem, *Asia de Joam de Barros. Década I* (1932), pp. lviii-lxvii, for relevant documentation. Pedro Paulo Ferrer, S.J. (1536-1618), a native of Malaga, taught for many years in the theological faculty of the Jesuit University at Evora after his arrival there in December 1559.
7. António Baião, *Documentos ineditos* (1917), pp. 112-113; *Ibidem*, *Asia* (1932), p. lxvii. Severim de Faria, *Discursos* (1624), fl. 46.
8. "da qual materia copiosamente tratamos em os livros da nossa Esfera da instructura das cousas, na parte mecanica, que he toda de arquitectura."
9. *Discursos* (1624), fl. 47 (misprinted, 45).

10. *Discursos* (1624) loc. cit.
11. Maria Leonor de Carvalhão Buescu, "Os *Grammaticos Rudimenta* de João de Barros", in *Arquivos do Centro Cultural Português,* Vol. IV (Paris, 1972), pp. 93-140.

8

SIGNIFICANCE AND CONTRIBUTION

Some indication of the interest which the work of João de Barros aroused in his lifetime and beyond has been given in the foregoing chapters, but a summary reconsideration will be in order here. As mentioned previously, Barros was frankly disappointed at the lack of recognition which his work achieved among his compatriots. He gave vent to his feelings in his "Apology by way of Prologue" to his (posthumous) *Decade IV*, which can be regarded as his literary testament. He complained that not only third parties, but even some of his own family and friends, had criticised him for spending so much time on writing books, and for neglecting to amass a fortune which his children could inherit. He reiterated, somewhat defensively, that all the writing of his books was done outside of office-hours, by burning the midnight oil, by working on High-days, Holidays and Feast-Days, by avoiding social entertainments and by declining invitations to hunting trips and fishing parties. He averred that foreigners appreciated his published works more than did his fellow-countrymen. He declared that in future he would concentrate on completing his Latin "World-Geography", which would be sure of a warm welcome abroad if not at home.[1]

Like many authors, João de Barros seems to have been unduly sensitive to criticism, and unduly dissatisfied with the amount of recognition which he did, in fact, receive in his lifetime. The first two *Decades* had been translated into Italian by Alfonso Ulloa and published at Venice in 1561-62, as Barros duly acknowledged. But he was apparently piqued that not only had Fernão Lopes de Castanheda pipped him to the post in 1551, but that his rival's eight Books had all appeared in print before his own *Decade III* was published, and that Castanheda's first Book had been translated into both French (1553) and Spanish (1554). He might have been still more annoyed if he had known that, after his own death, Ulloa would translate seven out of Castanheda's eight Books into Italian, while leaving the third *Decade* of Barros untranslated.[2]

Barros' complaints against his compatriots were not altogether well-founded, even though they were certainly justified up to a point. King John III and the royal family did not waver in their patronage of him, and he received more substantial monetary rewards than did many other good and faithful servants of the Lusitanian Crown. After the publication of *Decade I*, the king asked Barros to undertake the chronicle of his father, King Manuel. Barros accepted, expecting that he would be relieved of his onerous duties at the India House and given (paid) time off to work on this project. This did not happen, and he had too many literary irons in the fire to make any progress on writing the Chronicle. The task was then turned over to his great friend, Damião de Góis, involving the latter in serious trouble on the first publication of his *Chronicle of Dom Manuel* in 1566.[3]

We have seen that if some of the criticism directed at the *Decades* was malicious and irresponsible, some of it contained a core of truth; and his own attitude to Fernão Lopes de Castanheda was anything but generous. His friends and admirers included several of the leading Portuguese humanists of that Golden Age, Duarte de Resende, André de Resende, António Luis, and Damião de Góis. The last-named, in his memorial from prison to the Lisbon Inquisitors, dated 23 July 1572, referred to João de Barros as "one of the best friends that I ever had in this kingdom". Apart from these and other influential Portuguese humanists who could be named, Barros was on friendly terms with many of the leading personalities of the Court and the government bureaucracy. They included Dom António de Ataíde, Count of Castanheira, Comptroller of the Exchequer and one of King John III's most trusted and intimate counsellors; Dom João de Castro, the famous hero of Portuguese India; and Fernão Peres de Andrade, a pioneer of the China Trade, and Comptroller of the Lisbon Dockyard. The list could easily be extended.

If it be true that a man is known by his friends, then João de Barros had every reason to be satisfied with his.

Foreign recognition, as he himself acknowledged, was certainly not lacking. Pope Pius IV is said to have placed his bust or portrait next to that of Ptolomey in the Vatican, during his pontificate (1555-59). It is also claimed that he was awarded a similar honour at Venice. Unfortunately, whether bust or portrait, neither seems to have survived. Barros tells us that in 1549 he sent some of his Chinese and Persian books to the celebrated Italian humanist and historian, Paolo Govio (1483-1552), at the request of the Papal Nuncio at Lisbon and of Cardinal Farnese. He did so, he adds, because he did not wish to show himself niggardly in the use of his material; and he thought that Govio might be able to publish it sooner, since he was not distracted with the burden and responsibilities of a full-time bureaucratic job. Paolo Govio did in fact make use of this material in his classic *History of his own Times* (*Historia sui Temporis*, 1558), where he advanced the theory that the art of printing had travelled from China to Europe. Severim de Faria, however, complains that the Italian scholar made no specific acknowledgment of his indebtedness to João de Barros, but contented himself with a vague reference to Portuguese services in general.[4]

As mentioned previously, the Florentine humanist and merchant, Filippo Sassetti (1540-88), read and praised the *Decades* of João de Barros. It is significant, however, that although Sassetti had lived at Lisbon for four years (1578-81) before going out as a commercial agent for a group of Italian pepper contractors to Portuguese India, where he died, he does not mention any of the didactic and pedagogical works of Barros. It is also rather odd that he apparently did not know of Ulloa's Italian translation (1561-62) of the first two *Decades*, since he wrote to an unidentified correspondent : "Oh, how fine this work would be in any other language save Portuguese!" He praised Barros highly for his factual accuracy and geographical knowledge; but he criticised him for the trivial and boring details which he gave about numerous individual *fidalgos* and soldiers. Nevertheless, as we have seen, he acknowledged that such trivia were unavoidable when writing a work of this kind for the Portuguese reading public, since each and every one of them wanted to be ranked as a *fidalgo*, whatever his real social origins. Illiterate peasants and artisans did not scruple to take the names of aristocratic families, such as the Almeidas. Noronhas, and Menezes, with which they had no parentage whatever.[5]

Among Barros' humanist friends, both António Luís and Damião de Gois dedicated little Latin works to him. So did their more famous Spanish colleague, Luís Vicente Vives, in a eulogistic dedication to a treatise on mental prayer entitled *Exercitationum animi in Deum*, dated at Antwerp in August 1535.[6] We have seen (p. 30) that Richard Hakluyt referred to him approvingly in 1582; but of greater significance for the diffusion of his name and fame among the erudite reading public of the sixteenth century were the extracts from the first two *Decades* published in Italian translation by Giovanni Battista Ramusio (1485-1557) in his popular *Delle Navigationi e Viaggi* (3 vols, 1550-59-63 and subsequent editions).[7] In the 1554 edition of Vol. I (fls. 426-36) the great Venetian scholar published in Italian six chapters from the first *Decade* dealing with West Africa and India. Nevertheless, by the time of his death, Barros had achieved no more than a relatively modest international fame in the learned circles of Western Europe as a historian of Portuguese expansion in general, and more particularly as an authority on China. But his *Ropica Pnefma* and his pedagogical works seem to have been unread outside his own country, and they were largely ignored or forgotten within it. Jerónimo de Barros claimed that Shah Abbas the Great of Persia (reigned, 1587-1629) ordered a translation of the *Decades* to be made into that language. If so, I am not aware that anything ever came of it. Jerónimo himself is not an overly reliable witness; but the "Great Sophy" had an intelligent and inquiring mind, and it is possible that he at any rate contemplated such a project.[8]

The two trends which reflected the contemporary evaluation of Barros' works continued after his death. The *Decades* were used with or without acknowledgment by most European scholars who published works on Asia in general, and on China in particular, for the rest of the sixteenth and for most of the seventeenth centuries. A typical example is afforded by the 1577 *Discurso de la navegación que los Portugueses hazen a los Reinos y Provincias del Oriente, y de la noticia que se tiene de las grandezas del Reino de la China* of Bernardino de Escalante. But, as we have seen, the *Ropica Pnefma* was banned by the Portuguese Inquisition in 1581, and the educational and moral treatises had to wait until 1785 for another (and incomplete) edition.

Barros obviously thought that the sales of his *Decades* were sluggish during his lifetime; and this was certainly true after his death, despite recognition of their value by an evidently limited group of international scholars. Diogo do Couto, who was finally appointed Barros' official successor in 1595, two years later declared in the dedicatory preface to King Philip of his own fourth *Decade* : "The *Decades* of our compatriot, João de Barros, which are worthy of great estimation, both through his great learning as because of the great exploits which he recounted, were so little esteemed by our nation that there was no edition after the first, which has been so consumed by time, that I doubt if there are ten copies left in Portugal and even one in India".[9] Some commentators have taken this to mean that the *Decades* were in great demand; but the publication-history of the second edition shows that this was not so.

When João Baptista Lavanha published the composite fourth *Decade* in 1615, this edition was limited to 850 copies. Even so, it sold so slowly that the Lisbon Municipality, which had only reluctantly financed its publication at the insistence of the Crown (prodded by Lavanha), still had 350 copies on their hands eight years later. To get rid of these, they finally resolved (again after much prodding by the Crown and by Lavanha) to reprint the first three *Decades*, which they did in 1628, hence the name of "edition of the Senate", which is sometimes given to this set.[10] Lavanha's original contract only called for the printing of 500 copies of *Decade IV*, although he actually printed 350 extra, which may imply that the original edition of 1552-63 was limited to

500 copies of each volume. In any event, the *editio princeps* is unlikely to have exceeded a thousand copies of each one.

It is evident that the *Decades* were admired, rather than read, for centuries. The modest 1628 edition together with the composite *Decade IV* of 1615 clearly satisfied what limited demand there was. A new edition was not called for until 1777, although an isolated reprint of *Decade I*, dedicated to an English merchant, John Bristow, was published at Lisbon in 1752. In 1621, Dom Fernando Alvia de Castro, "Muster-Master of the Royal Armada and Army of the Ocean Sea, and of the military and naval force of the kingdom of Portugal", published a little collection of sententious aphorisms culled from the first *Decade* of João de Barros. He promised to follow this up with a further collection taken from the second and third *Decades*, if there was a sufficient response from the reading public to his preliminary effort. There was nothing of the kind, and no continuation appeared.[11]

Foreign appreciation of the works of João de Barros was likewise confined to the *Decades* and was on a relatively modest scale for centuries. Extracts from the *Decades* were included in most collections of travel literature, such as Melchisedec Thevenot's *Relations des Voyages* of 1696, and in the Dutch publisher-bookseller, Pieter van der Aa's *Doorluchtige Scheeps-togten der Portugysen na Oost-Indien, Africa etc.* (Leiden, 1707-1727); but a translation of all four *Decades* had to wait until the appearance of a 5-volume German version in 1821.

Although always highly considered by a discerning minority of scholarly readers, the *Decades* only secured wider recognition within the last hundred years. It is safe to say that their prestige has never been higher than at present, and this is reflected in the prevailing market-prices for the 1552-1777 editions. This makes it all the more regrettable that there is no annotated translation of any of the *Decades* in English, and that a project for such an edition of *Decade I* by the Hakluyt Society has been abandoned.[12] When Fray Mariano Azaro claimed in 1583 that João de Barros was the best-informed man who had ever lived, the worthy Carmelite friar was obviously exaggerating. But the Portuguese humanist and historian was certainly one of the best informed men of his Age in Western Europe, and his work is deserving of wider recognition in the wider world. If this little book helps to make him better known, it will have achieved its object.

NOTES

1. "E porque nesta parte estou mais obrigado aos estranhos, que a elles [Portugueses,] por lhe serem meus trabalhos mais aceptos, pera os satisfazer no que esperam de mim, converto a minha penna a estes, que me querem, escrevendo a Geographia de todo o Orbe descuberto, e as gentes delle".
2. For the original editions and those in translation see Francis Rogers (ed.). *Europe Informed. An Exhibition of Early Books which acquainted Europe with the East* (Cambridge, Mass. New York, 1966), pp. 51-53, 55-58.
3. Severim de Faria, *Discursos* (1624), fl. 38; Elizabeth Hirsch, *Damião de Gois, 1502-1574* (1967), pp. 171-72, 202-03.
4. *Decade I*, Book 9, ch, i; Severim de Faria, *Discursos* (1624).
5. *Lettere di Filippo Sassetti sopra i soui Viaggi nelle Indie Orientali dal 1578 al 1588* (Reggio, 1844), pp. 222-30, especially p. 223, On Filippo Sassetti see Donald Lach, *Asia in the making of Europe*, index *in voce*.
6. L. Vives, *Opera in duos distincta Tomos* (2 vols., Basel, 1555), Vol. II, pp. 199-206. I owe this reference to my friend and colleague, Luís de Sousa Rebello.
7. Gian Battista Ramusio, *Navigationi et Viaggi, 1563-1606* (eds. R.A. Skelton, George B. Parks, 3 vols., Amsterdam, 1970), Vol. III (1970), p. 16 for the six chapters which Ramusio took from *Decade I*, and printed for the first time in 1554 (reprinted, 1563, 1588, and later editions). Cf. also A Teixeira da Mota, "A Africa Ocidental em Os Lusíadas" in *Garcia d' Orta Numero Especial* (Lisboa, 1972), pp. 381-92, for the debt of Camoes to Barros.
8. ". . . sey que ora é da Persia a manda agora tradozir em lingoa parsia". . . (*apud* A. Baião, *Documentos inéditos*, p. 113).
9. Diogo do Couto, *Decada Quarta da Asia* (Lisboa, 1602), fl, 2 of the dedicatory epistle to Philip I of Portugal (II of Spain) d. Goa, 20 Nov 1597.
10. See the documents printed by A. Baião, *Asia de Joam de Barros* (1932), pp. lxxii-lxxx.
11. *Aphorismos, y exemples politicos y militares sacados de la primera Decada de Juan de Barros. Por Don Fernando Alvia de Castro,*

Provedor de la Real Armada y Exercito del Mar Oceano, y de la gente de guerra del Reyno de Portugal (Lisboa, 1621). He lists a total of 379 examples.

12. More especially as the projected editors, Professor G.W.L. Randles and the late Senhor Freire de Andrade, were eminently suited for this challenging task.

ADDENDUM TO BIBLIOGRAPHY

As explained above (p. 8), this work was originally completed in 1973, and bibliographical references have been updated only in a few places. Readers wishing to pursue the study of João de Barros in more depth should start with the admirable work of Dr. José V. de Pina Martins, *Humanismo e Erasmismo na cultura Portuguesa do século XVI. Estudo e Textos* (Fundação Calouste Gulbenkian, Centro Cultural Português, Paris, 1973). They can continue by consulting the invaluable *Arquivos* published by the same institution under the direction of Dr. José V. de Pina Martins, which are still in progress and which contain many relevant articles on Portuguese Humanism in all its aspects.

It should also be added for the benefit of those who are not at home in German, that an excellent English translation by Fr. M. Joseph Costelloe S.J., of the late Fr. Georg Schurhammer S.J.'s monumental biography of St. Francis Xavier is now in progress. Three volumes have already appeared under the title of *St. Francis Xavier. His Life, His Times* (Jesuit Historical Institute, Rome, 1973-80). Similarly, three more volumes, misleadingly labelled as "Books", of Professor Donald F. Lach's *Asia in the Making of Europe* (Chicago University Press), have been published since 1973, thus completing this invaluable analytical survey of European literature on Asia during the sixteenth century.

Reference item 12 below (p. 150), *Decada* II has now been reprinted with an introduction by Professor Lindley F. Cintra (Lisboa, Casa da Moeda, 1974).

BIBLIOGRAPHY

A. *Works of João de Barros, 1522-1615.*
(*Arranged in chronological order*).

1. *Prymera parte da cronica do emperador Clarimundo donde os Reys de Portugal descendem.*
(Lisboa, Germao Galharde, 3 Março 1522).
Anselmo nr. 567.
Second edition published at Coimbra by João de Barreira, 5 July 1555.
Anselmo nr. 138.
Other editions : Lisboa, 1601, 1742, 1791, 1843; and the 3-volume edition in the Clássicos Sá da Costa by Professor Marques Braga, Lisboa, 1953, which is that mainly used here, although the 1555 edition has also been consulted.
2. *Ropicapnefma de João de Barros* (Lisboa, Germao Galharde, 8 May 1532).
Anselmo nr. 596.
Reprinted in an inaccurate and very limited edition by the Visconde de Azevedo (Porto, 1869).
João de Barros. Ropica Pnefma, Reprodução facsimilada da edição de 1532. Leitura modernizada, notas e estudo de I. S. Révah. (2 vols. Lisboa, Instituto de Alta Cultura. Centro de Estudos de Psicologia e de História da Filosofia anexo à Faculdade de Letras da Universidade de Lisboa, (1952-55). Vol. I contains the facsimile, Vol. II the introduction and modernized text. The notes (Vol. 3), were never published).
3. *Panegirico do Rei D. João III*
Delivered at Evora in 1533.
First published in the second edition of Manuel Severim de Faria, *Notícias de Portugal* (Oficına de António Isidoro da Fonseca, Lisboa, 1740), and not in the first

edition of 1655, as erroneously stated by Sra. Maria Leonor Carvalhão Buescu p. 31 of her *Textos Pedagógicos e Gramaticas de João de Barros* (Editorial Verbo, Lisboa, 1969).

This 1740 edition is full of errors and omissions, and another in 1791 is not much better. I have used the definitive edition by M. Rodrigues Lapa in his *João de Barros. Panegíricos. Texto restituido, prefácio e notas* in the series Clássicos Sá da Costa (2nd ed., Lisboa, 1943), pp. 1-160.

4. *Panegírico da mui alta e esclarecida princesa Infanta Dona Maria Nossa Senhora.*
   Delivered in 1535.
   First published in the first edition of Manuel Severim de Faria, *Notícias de Portugal* (Lisboa, 1655), pp. 306-342.
   Reprinted in 1791. I have used the definitive edition by M. Rodrigues Lapa in his *João de Barros. Panegíricos texto restituido, prefácio e notas*, in the series Clássicos Sá da Costa (2nd ed., Lisboa, 1943), pp. 161-219.
5. *Grammatica da lingua portuguesa com os mandamentos da santa mádre igreja*, usually described from the title given to it in the wording of the colophon, as *Cartinha com os preceitos e mandamentos da santa madre igreja, e com os misterios da missa e responsorios della* (Lisboa, Luís Rodrigues, 22 December 1539).
   Anselmo, nr. 1005.
   Reprinted in the *Compilaçã) de varias obros do insigne portuguez Joam de Barros, dirigidas pelo mesmo autor ao muito alto, e excellente Principe D. Felipe. Impressas em Lisboa em Caza de Luiz Rodriguez Livreiro d'El Rey, pelos annos de 1539 e 1540. E agora reimpressas em beneficio público pelos Monges da Real Cartucha de N.S. da Escada do Ceo* (Lisboa, Na Officina de Jozé da Silva Nazareth, 1785), pp. 1-67.
   This defective edition has now been replaced by the 1971 edition edited by Maria Leonor Carvalhão Buescu, q.v.
6. *Grammatica da lingua Portugesa* (Olyssipone. Apud Lodouicum Rotorigiu Typographum. M.D.X.L.) At fl. 50v.

begins the "Dialogo em louvor da nossa linguagem", ending on fl. 60v.

Reprinted in the *Compilação de varias obras* (1785), pp. 69-237, in an unsatisfactory edition.

The *Gramática* (less the *Diálogo*) had a third and scrupulous edition by José Pedro Machado, Lisboa, 1957, but from the average reader's point of view, the best and most convenient is that by Maria Leonor Carvalhão Buescu (q.v.) in 1971. The *Diálogo* alone has been several times reprinted, including a scholarly version by Luciana Stegagno Picchio, *João de Barros. Diálogo em louvor da nossa linguagem. Lettura critica dell' edizione del 1540 con una introduzione su la questione della lingua in Portogallo* (Modena, 1959).

7. *Dialogo da uiciosa Vergonha* (Olyssippone. Apud Lodouicum Rotorigiu Typographum M.D.X.L. The Colophon is dated 12 January 1540).

   Anselmo nr. 1011.

   Reprinted in the *Compilacao de varias obras* (1785), pp. 239-340; and in extracts and with a commentary by Maria Leonor Carvalhão Buescu, *Textos Pedagógicos e Gramaticais de João de Barros* (1969).

   The most satisfactory edition is that by Maria Leonor Carvalhão Buescu (1971), q.v.

8. *Dialogo de preceitos morães cõ prática delles, em modo de iogo* (Lisboa, Luís Rodriguez, 27 March 1540).

   Reproduced in photo-facsimile with short but valuable commentary by José F. da Silva Terra, *L'édition princeps du Dialogo de Preceitos moraes de João de Barros*, reprinted from the *Bulletin des Etudes Portugais* of the Institut Français au Portugal, Nouvelle Série, Voi. XXX, pp. 77-87 which is the edition used here.

   For the second edition published by João Barreira at Lisbon on the 20 August 1563, see Anselmo nr. 172. Reprinted by the Visconde de Azevedo in a very limited and not entirely trustworthy edition in his continuation of the *Compilação* in 1869, for which see Silva Terra, op. cit., pp. 81-82.

9. *Grammatices Rudimenta.*
Written in or about the year 1540, the beautifully illuminated contemporary copy of this unfinished MS. has now been published by Maria Leonor Carvalhão Buescu "Os *Grammatices Rudimenta* de João de Barros", in Fundação Calouste Gulbenkian, *Arquivos do Centro Cultural Português*, Vol. IV (Paris, 1972), pp. 93-140.
See also the article by Justino Mendes de Almeida, "Uma Gramática Latina de João de Barros", in *Euphrosyne*, Vol. II (Lisboa, 1959), pp, 255-62.

10. *Diálogo Evangelico sobre os artigos da Fé contra o Talmud dos Judeus.*
Written *c.* 1542-43, it was first published with a learned introduction and notes by I.S. Révah (Lisboa, Livraria Studium Editora, 1950), which is the edition used here.

11. *Asia de Joam de Barros dos fectos que os Portugueses fizeram no descobrimento e conquista dos mares e terras do Oriente* (Lisboa, Germão Galharde, 28 June 1552).
Anselmo, nr. 648.
Segunda decada da Asia de Joã de Barros dos feitos que os Portugueses fizeram no descobrimẽto e cõquista dos mares e terras do oriente (Lisboa, Germão Galharde, 24 March 1553).
Anselmo nr. 648.
Terceira decada da Asia de Ioam de Barros: Dos feytos que os Portugueses fizeram no descobrimẽnto e conquista dos mares e terras do Oriente (Lisboa, Ioam de Barreira, 28 August 1563).
Anselmo nr. 176.
These first three *Decades* were reprinted in the so-called "edition of the Senate" by Jorge Rodrigues, 3 vols., Lisboa, 1628.

12. *Quarta Decada da Asia de Ioao de Barros Dos feitos que os Portugueses fizerão no descobrimento e conquista dos mares e terras do Oriente* (Madrid, Impressão Real, 1615). Edited by João Baptista Lavanha.
These first editions of 1552-1615 are the only really trustworthy texts. The commonly used 9-volume reprint edition of 1777-78 leaves something to be desired, and the

4-volume edition (Lisboa, Agência Geral das Colonias, 1944-47) is even worse.

There was a reprint of *Decada* I in 1752, which I have not bothered to consult, since I used the first edition of 1552.

An acceptable reprint of *Decada* I was made by António Baião in 1932 (Coimbra University), but it has no notes and it is not 100% reliable.

B. *Secondary Works and Background Material.*

13. Anselmo, António, Joaquim. *Bibliografia das obras impressas em Portugal no século XVI* (Lisboa: Biblioteca Nacional, 1926). Requires updating in some respects, but is still the best and fullest bibliography of books published in 16th century Portugal and essential for any study of the intellectual background.

14. Baião, António. *Documentos inéditos sôbre João de Barros. Sôbre o escritor seu homónimo contemporâneo, sôbre a família do historiador e sôbre os continuadores das suas "Decadas"* (Coimbra, Imprensa da Universidade, 1917). Reprint edition from the Academia das Sciências de Lisboa, *Boletim da Segunda Classe*, Vol. XI.

    Extracts from this edition and some new documentation were published by A. Baião in the lengthy introduction (pp. v-lxxxii) of his 1932 edition of *Decada* I (q.v. under Barros *Supra*), and again in the preface to his edition of selections from the *Decadas* in the Clássicos Sá da Costa edition, 4 vols., 195?.

    My quotations are from the 1917 and 1932 editions.

15. Bataillon, Marcel, *Etudes sur le Portugal au temps de l'humanisme* (Coimbra University Press, 1952). Collection of articles by one of the outstanding scholars in the field of Humanism and the Renaissance.

16. Carvalhão Buescu, Maria Leonor. *Textos Pedagógicos e Gramaticais de João de Barros. Introdução, Selecção, notas e leitura* (Lisboa Editorial Verbo, 1969).

    A useful introduction for the beginner.

17. Carvalhão Buescu, Maria Leonor. *João de Barros. Gramática da Lingua Portuguesa. Cartinha, Gramática, Diálogo em louvor da nossa linguagem e diálogo da Viçiosa Vergonha. Reprodução facsimilada, leitura, introdução e anotações.*

(Faculdade de Letras da Universidade de Lisboa, 1971). Excellent edition, which supersedes all the previous ones of these works by João de Barros.

18. Castello-Branco, Fernando, "Cartilhas Quinbentistas para ensinar a ler", in Fundação Calouste Gulbenkian : Centro de investigação pedagógica, *Boletim bibliográfico e informativo.* Vol. 14 (Lisboa, 1971), pp. 109-152.
——"——, "Portugal Quinhentista visto através das cartilhas para ensinar a ler", in *Anais da Academia Portuguesa da História,* II Serie, Vol. 21 (Lisboa, 1972). Two well-illustrated and well-documented analyses of these *cartilhas,* and evaluating the exceptional importance of that by João de Barros.
19. Cidade, Hernâni. *Portugal Histórico-Cultural* (2d. edition, Lisboa, Editora Arcadia Ltda., 1968). Contains a stimulating article, "João de Barros, o historiador da Expansão" (pp. 121-66).
20. Cortez Pinto, Américo. *Da Famosa Arte da Imprimissão. Da Impressa em Portugal ás Cruzdas d'Alem-Mar* (Lisboa, Editora Ulisseia Ltda, 1948) pp. 357-61, for the Tamil-Portuguese catechism and João de Barros. This catechism is now accessible in a facsimile edition.
Cartilha em Tamul e Português. Impressa em 1554 por ordem do Rei. Edição Fac-Simile do Museu Nacional de Arqueologia e Etnologia com preambulo de D. Fernando de Almeida (Ministério da Educação Nacional, Direcção-Geral do Ensino Superior e das Belas-Artes, Lisboa, 1970).
21. Espinosa Gomes da Silva, Nuno J. *Humanismo e direito em Portugal no século XVI* (Lisboa, 1964).
An excellent discussion of Humanism and the Renaissance in Portugal from an unusual perspective, including João de Barros' criticisms of the law and of lawyers in *Ropica Pnefma* (pp. 96-109).
22. Hirsch, Elisabeth Feist. *Damião de Gois. The life and thought of a Portuguese Humanist, 1502-1574.*
(The Hague, M. Nijhoff, 1967).
For those who cannot read Portuguese or French, this is the best English-language work concerned with Humanism and the Renaissance in Portugal.

23. Lach, Donald F. *Asia in the making of Europe*, I, *The Century of Discovery* (Books I and II, in two volumes numbered consecutively to form one. University of Chicago Press, 1965). An excellent synthesis of sixteenth century printed European works on Asia, in which the *Decades* of Barros are given their rightful prominence and are used to the best effect.

24. Matos, Luís de, *Les Portugais à l'Université de Paris entre 1500 et 1550.* (Coimbra UP, 1950).
Biographical details on many of the Portuguese students who attended the University of Paris during this period, with some discussion of their influence. Complemented by the work of Joaquim Verissimo Serrão, *Les Portugais à l'Université de Toulouse, XIII-XVII siècles* (Paris, 1970).

25. Révah, Israel Salvator. *La Censure Inquisitoriale Portugaise au XVIe siècle. Etude accompagnée de la reproduction en fac-simile des Index*, Vol. I [all published] (Lisboa, Centro de Estudos de Psicologia e de História da Filosofia anexo à Faculdade de Letras da Universidade de Lisboa, 1960). The best study of the subject to date, unfortunately not continued by the author before his death.
For Révah's editions of the *Ropica Pnefma* and *Diálogo Evangelico* see under Barros above.
Of the numerous relevant articles by Révah perhaps the two most fundamental are: "Le Colloque *Ropicapnefma* de João de Barros, Genèse, Structure et Technique" (*Bulletin Hispanique*, Vol. LXIV *bis*, *Mélanges offerts à Marcel Bataillon par les Hispanistes Français*, Bordeaux, 1962, pp. 571-592), and the later "Antiquité et Christianisme, 'Anciens et Modernes' dans l'oeuvre de João de Barros" *Revue Philosophique de la France et de l'Etranger*, Paris, 1966, pp. 165-85). There is a marked shift in his viewpoint, the 1966 article being much less favourable to Barros, but I find the first more convincing.

26. Saraiva António José. *História da Cultura em Portugal* (3 vols., Lisboa, Jornal do Foro, 1950-62). Volumes 2 and 3 of this often controversial but always stimulating work are particularly useful, devoting, as they do, much

space to an analysis of the *Ropica Pnefma* and the *Decades* of João de Barros.

27. Severim de Faria, Manuel. *Discursos varios Politicos* (Evora, 1624). Fls. 22-59 (some of them misnumbered), "Vida de Ioao de Barros", is still the basic biography, on which all later ones are built.

28. Silva Dias, José Sebastião da. *A Política Cultural da época de D. João III*, Vol. I (in two parts, with continuous pagination. University of Coimbra Press, 1969).
All published at the time of this writing (Sept. 1973), this massive and densely documented work is essential reading for anyone seriously studying 16th century Portuguese culture and intellectual life. Pp. 253-86 are devoted to João de Barros, who also receives frequent mention *passim*.
The same author's earlier *Correntes de Sentimento Religioso em Portugal* (*séculos XVI a XVIII*), (1 volume—in 2 parts with continuous pagination, Coimbra U.P., 1960) is devoted entirely to the 16th century and is also very useful in its more limited sphere.

29. Silva Dias, José Sebastião da. *Os Descobrimentos e a problemática cultural do século XVI* (Universidade de Coimbra, 1973).
Discusses the influence of the Portuguese and Spanish overseas expansion in a European as well as an Iberian context. Barros frequently cited (index, *in voce*).

30. Sousa Rebelo, Luis de. "Armas e Letras", in João José Cochofel (ed.) *Grande Dicionário da Literatura Portuguesa e de Teoria Literária*, Vol. I, pp. 426-52 (Lisboa, Iniciativas Editoriais, 1973).
Received after this Manuscript was finished in 1973, Rebelo's article contains a most penetrating analysis of the relevant passages in *Ropica Pnefma* and the *Diálogos*. It must be consulted by any serious student of this problem and of João de Barros.

31. Stegagno Picchio, Luciana. *João de Barros. Diálogo em louvor da nossa linguagem. Lettura critica dell'edizione del 1540 con una introduzione su la Questione della Lingua in Portogallo* (Modena, Societa' Tipografica Editrice

Modense, 1959). Excellent little study although I.S. Révah pointed out in a review: "l'éditeur n'a pas tenu compte dans l'établissement du texte, du système d'accentuation des voyelles toniques inventé par João de Barros en 1539-40" (*Bulletin des Etudes Portugaises*, Vol. XXII, 1959-60, p. 308).

32. Van Royen, Theda. "Contribuito para a revisão do conceito erasmismo e a sua influencia na literatura portuguesa do século XVI com base na Ropica Pnefma de João de Barros", in *Ocidente*, Vol. LXXIII, nr. 354, (Lisboa, 1967), pp. 1-36 of the *Supplemento*.
She is rather scornful of João de Barros, claiming that Gil Vicente was much more effective and outspoken as a social critic, and that Barros was rather muddled and unoriginal in "Ropica Pnefma", finding himself in a blind alley ("beco sem saida").

33. Vasconcellos, Carolina Michäelis de. *A Infanta D. Maria de Portugal, 1521-1571, e as suas damas* (Porto. 1902). Still the definitive study of the educated ladies at the Court of Portugal at the high tide of the Portuguese Renaissance.

INDEX